Chris Ak~~erman~~ and worked
in the UK, Belgium and Australia before becoming a teacher
at the University of Surrey. This is his first book.

WITHDRAWN

Constable & Robinson Ltd
55–56 Russell Square
London WC1B 4HP
www.constablerobinson.com

First published in the UK by How To Books,
an imprint of Constable & Robinson Ltd, 2014

A copy of the British Library Cataloguing in
Publication data is available from the British Library

ISBN 978-1-47211-037-4 (paperback)
ISBN 978-1-84528-555-5 (ebook)

Printed and bound in the UK

1 3 5 7 9 10 8 6 4 2

BEST MAN'S DUTIES

Chris Akerman

howtobooks

CONTENTS

1. INTRODUCTION

1.1 ACCEPTING THE HONOUR

Being chosen by someone to be his best man is a great honour and no doubt you feel proud to have been asked. However, I expect that, quite soon, in my case it was a matter of moments, you began to realise the full implications. You are going to have to stand up at the wedding reception and give an entertaining speech. This can have a very sobering effect, literally for me. When I was asked, the groom and I had just been out for a few beers and I was halfway through my curry when the bombshell was dropped.

As well as the speech, there is the stag party to organise, which can appear a daunting prospect, particularly as the options available and complexity seem to increase every year. In addition, there are all the other smaller tasks that come under the remit of the best man, plus providing general support to the groom throughout the whole process. Pretty soon you may feel a bit overwhelmed and start to wonder how you can get out of it. Well, I'm afraid that is generally not an option, as in this case the groom is like Don Corleone in *The Godfather*: he has made you an offer you can't refuse.

By now you will be beginning to realise the wide variety of skills the best man needs to possess: organisation and administration, speech writing, public speaking, counselling, diplomacy and decision making. Combine all these requirements with the fact that the job is unpaid and you can see why there's no point in the groom advertising it in the hope of attracting willing and qualified applicants. However, there are a couple of redeeming features that make it a worthwhile role for whoever takes it on. First, it's a privilege and an honour to be asked, and second, you get a great sense of achievement when it all goes well on the day. The groom has chosen you not just because you are a close friend, but because he clearly feels that you have most, or perhaps all, of the above skills. This is quite a compliment and one very good reason why you should feel confident in your ability to do the job well.

In addition, this book will help you rise to the challenge, and, as former US President Franklin D. Roosevelt once said: 'The only thing we have to fear is fear itself' (as an aside, quotes are extremely useful things to include in your speech so I will be using lots of them when we get on to talking about the speech in detail later in this book). Most importantly, you have one great weapon on your side and that is time. That's assuming that the original best man hasn't had to pull out at the last minute and you are reading this on the night before the wedding, in which case fear is probably the appropriate feeling. I remember on the day before my own wedding, when the best man didn't arrive on the expected train and we couldn't get hold of him, I asked the chief usher if he would stand in, if necessary, and although we cannot publish what he did say, it certainly wasn't 'sure, no problem'!

The time that you have will allow you to plan everything that you need to do for the wedding, so that you can feel completely in control, not panic, and enjoy the experience of being the groom's best man.

1.2 HOW THIS BOOK WILL HELP

Having been through the experience of being a best man I know just how much I would have appreciated a practical and comprehensive guide to support me at the time, which is exactly what this book is intended to provide.

The best man's responsibilities can be divided into three main areas that will be addressed by this book. These are the stag party, the speech and other duties. I have given a summary of each area of responsibility below.

THE STAG PARTY (CHAPTER 4)

The best man is responsible for organising the stag party, and all the options are comprehensively explored in Chapter 4. These range from a simple night out at the local pub, through to a full weekend of activities abroad. Online references have been provided to enable you to follow up on all the ideas discussed.

Having decided on what to do, when to do it and whom to invite with your groom, you will then be responsible for organising the event. This is no simple administrative task for it involves contacting invitees, making bookings (for transport, accommodation, activities), collecting money, making payments and organising everyone on the day/weekend itself. So unless you happen to work in the events industry you are going to find this role challenging. This chapter will help you through the whole process and ensure you remain organised and the event goes smoothly. Of course what I cannot do for you is help with your most important task, which is to look after the groom and make sure he comes home in one piece. When I mentioned to a friend that I was writing this book, she immediately told me the story of her friend's husband, who on his stag night climbed onto, and then promptly fell off, the roof of a double-decker bus and spent the wedding day with his jaw sewn up! No doubt there are many other stories of stag-night accidents, so make sure that your groom doesn't end up as a cautionary tale in the next edition of this book.

THE SPEECH (CHAPTERS 6–8)

Anyone who is asked to be a best man will naturally be apprehensive (almost certainly an understatement) at the thought of having to prepare and deliver an amusing speech on the wedding day. These chapters guide you through the whole process of preparing and delivering the speech.

Chapter 6 will give you lots of practical guidance on how to construct an entertaining speech personally tailored to your groom. It's important to consider the audience, so that the humour is appropriate, and there will be a discussion on how to pitch your speech at the right level. Although you probably know the groom very well, there are always things to be discovered from family and other friends which could be good sources of material for the speech, so there will be guidance on what to look for and how to use it for comic effect. Chapter 6 also looks at what to include in each part of the speech, including how to get going at the start, what to include in the main section, and how to end on a high. Examples of props and quotes to use will be given, as will details of the toast to make at the end. Chapter 7 then has ten original sample speeches, which will be an invaluable source of material to you; seeing full-length speeches gives you a real feel for how to structure your own speech.

Having addressed the preparation of the speech, guidance will be given in Chapter 8 on how to deliver it successfully. This includes hints on practising and memorising your speech, overcoming nerves, delivery style and the use of body language. Therefore, having worked through these chapters you should be fully prepared to stand up confidently on the wedding day and give a great speech.

OTHER DUTIES (CHAPTERS 3 AND 5)

As best man you will probably be unsure exactly what other duties, in addition to the stag party and the speech, you must take responsibility for. These duties are fully explained in two chapters. The first deals with responsibilities arising before the wedding day itself (Chapter 3). For instance, as well as organising the stag party, you must ensure that your attire for the day (for both yourself and the groom) is arranged, you attend any pre-wedding gatherings and rehearsals and have sorted out where you and the groom will be staying the night before the wedding. Then the duties on the wedding day, other than the speech itself, are detailed in Chapter 5. There are many of these, including organising the ushers, possibly acting as Master of Ceremonies and looking after the rings. When I was best man, the groom was worried about losing the rings so he decided that it would be safer if he held onto them until we were inside the church. Anyway, we were about to go into the church when I spotted something shining on the ground in the car park. Without realising it, he had dropped the rings when he got out of the car! That anecdote of course went straight into my speech.

Before reading the chapters mentioned above detailing all your duties, it is useful as a best man to understand the bigger picture and where your role fits in, so in Chapter 2 the overall wedding process is explained. This includes an overview of what activities are carried out before the wedding and what happens on the day itself, including some background on the ceremony. It gives you an understanding of what is going on, which will enable you to provide the groom with encouraging words of support and advice when needed on more general matters relating to the wedding and also hopefully give you a sense of relief that, compared to organising the whole wedding, your own role is quite manageable.

In summary I hope that you find the detailed guidance given in this book useful in helping you to fulfil your role as best man with confidence and that, in doing so, you enjoy the experience.

2. WEDDINGS –
THE BIG PICTURE

2.1 INTRODUCTION

One of the best man's duties is to provide general support and advice to the groom before and on the wedding day itself. To help fulfil this role it is useful to have an overview of all aspects of the wedding; this knowledge will also allow you to see more clearly how your specific duties fit into the whole process. This chapter provides you with the bigger picture.

Before getting into the detail of the preparations for the wedding I should mention the type of wedding I have focused on in this chapter. For want of a better description I will call it a 'traditional white wedding', by which I mean one where the ceremony is followed by a reception which starts with drinks, then has a meal with speeches, and finishes with an evening party. This is the most popular wedding format in the UK, but even if the wedding you are attending varies in some respects, I hope that there are still some common elements that will make this chapter of help to you.

The traditional white wedding discussed is one where the groom appoints a best man and there are also bridesmaids, including a chief bridesmaid (also referred to as the maid of honour, if single, and the matron of honour, if married), and ushers (also referred to as groomsmen). I have used the name 'best man' for the chief attendant to the groom in this book whether the best man is a he or a she, as that person could also be a close female friend.

In addition it is possible to have more than one best man. This can be a solution when the groom finds it hard to decide between two close friends or would perhaps like to choose both his brother and another best friend. I have attended weddings where there have been two best men and they either delivered the speech as a double act or each one has given a separate short speech. Equally, one of the best men might be nominated to speak on behalf of them both. In this case perhaps the other best man would take on the responsibility of organising the stag party. I have heard of occasions when there have been three best men, although with that many, everyone would have to be very well organised indeed to ensure that tasks don't fall between the gaps and get overlooked.

In July 2013 the Marriage (Same Sex Couples) Act received royal assent, legalising marriage between same-sex couples in England and Wales, with the first marriages expected to take place by mid-2014 (marriage law in Scotland and Northern Ireland is the responsibility of the respective devolved governments, and at the time of writing a bill to introduce appropriate legislation legalising same-sex marriage in Scotland is currently passing through the Scottish parliament). Prior to this, the alternative to marriage for a same-sex couple was to enter into a civil partnership. Under the new legislation, partners currently in a civil partnership will have the option to convert it into a marriage if they so wish. Although this book is focused on mixed gender weddings, I hope it also provides useful information if you are a best man celebrating a civil partnership or, by the time you read this, a marriage between a same-sex couple.

2.2 TYPES OF CEREMONY

RELIGIOUS CEREMONY

There are many different religious wedding ceremonies carried out in the UK including Christian, Muslim, Hindu, Sikh, Jewish and Buddhist. Usually if the religious ceremony is performed by a person authorised to register marriages there is no need for a separate civil ceremony as the marriage is registered at the same time. As the most common religious ceremony in the UK is the Church of England ceremony (Office for National Statistics www.ons.gov.uk), I have discussed this in more detail in this chapter.

CIVIL CEREMONY

According to the Office for National Statistics, over two-thirds of couples marrying in England and Wales now have civil ceremonies. These ceremonies contain no religious element and can take place in a register office or any other approved premises licensed for civil marriages. Types of approved premises include hotels and stately homes, and according to the Office of National Statistics over half of all marriages in England and Wales now take place in these buildings. Some couples arrange to have a religious blessing after the civil ceremony, which is common when the bride or groom (or both) has been married before.

Another option is to have a humanist wedding after a civil ceremony. Humanist weddings have no legal status in England and Wales, hence the need to first have a civil ceremony, but they do have a legal status in Scotland, one of only a few countries in the world where this is the case. This type of wedding offers those couples without religious beliefs a very flexible alternative to create a ceremony with music, readings and vows closely tying into their own values.

2.3 BEFORE THE WEDDING DAY

INTRODUCTION

A wedding requires an incredible amount of planning; the best man's role in this is mainly to provide sympathetic support to the groom. Usually the three key people involved in the decision-making process in relation to planning the wedding day are the bride, the groom and the mother of the bride, with the chief bridesmaid providing the first line of support. Often the mother of the groom is also involved in decisions, and the fathers of the bride and groom may play some part in the preparations as well.

Sadly the best man cannot relax at this stage, as although you are unlikely to be involved in too much of the detailed decision-making, you may have to lend support to the groom while he struggles to make the right decision in areas where he almost certainly lacks the required level of expertise – for instance, if he has been asked to choose between edible favours, candle favours, or edible candle favours. However, if he is foolish enough to ask your opinion on this type of question my advice is that you try to establish the bride's view on the matter first before answering. This is one good reason to get to know the chief bridesmaid as soon as possible.

So, to help you fulfil your role, here is a summary of the preparations that will take place prior to the wedding day itself. Before making any major decisions the couple will doubtless first establish what sort of budget they have for the wedding and roughly how this might be spent on the different elements. They can then use this as a starting point for keeping track of costs as they go along. Parents may or may not be contributing to the wedding costs and this will affect the decision-making process. Traditionally, the bride's parents paid for the majority of the wedding costs, but it's now far more common for these to be shared, with the bride and groom, bride's parents and the groom's parents all contributing in some way. Having established a budget, the key decisions on the ceremony and reception venues will be made and the date set. Most of the other activities detailed below don't need to be done in a specific order.

CEREMONY AND RECEPTION VENUES

The couple will first need to decide whether to have a religious or civil ceremony. Having agreed on this, they will then consider the location for the ceremony and reception. If a Church of England ceremony is chosen, this will usually take place in the couple's local parish or one to which they have a particular connection, maybe where the bride's parents live.

The choice for the reception venue will probably be a hotel or something similar not too far from the church. Alternatively, if space allows, the bride and the groom may decide to hold the reception in a marquee in the garden of the bride's parents' home.

In the case of a civil wedding the ceremony can take place at a register office followed by a reception at a different venue, but it's now more common for the ceremony and reception to be held at the same approved premises. This reduces the level of organisation required and allows a smooth transition from ceremony to reception. A combined venue also means one less task for the best man on the day, as one of his duties is to make sure everyone has transport from the ceremony to the reception venue.

The choice of location for a civil ceremony grows every year and there are now some quite unusual locations in which to get married. For instance, as well as hotels and stately homes the couple could get married at sports grounds, castles, museums, zoos, railway stations, barns or even at a working lighthouse in Wales (www.trinityhouse.co.uk/lighthouses). However, there are some rules: in England and Wales you can only get married in a building which is open to the public, so that excludes most people's private homes. Also, couples must get married in some sort of permanent structure, so although this excludes getting married on the beach, they can marry in a gazebo in the grounds of approved premises. The law in Scotland on the other hand is more relaxed, and there you can get married in your home or outside, although it would take a brave couple to plan an outdoor wedding in Scotland! In

Northern Ireland religious weddings can take place anywhere, although civil marriages are either performed at a register office or at an approved place.

Until recently, marriages could only take place between 8 a.m. and 6 p.m. (although there were no restrictions in Scotland and Northern Ireland), but the law was changed in 2012 and in England and Wales couples can now get married at any time of the day or night, although ceremony venues can retain the traditional hours if they wish.

Once decided, and once the availability of both the ceremony and reception venues is confirmed, the date for the wedding can be set. The couple might at this point book accommodation at the venue or nearby hotels for the members of the wedding party; also the best man and the groom should decide where they will stay the night before the wedding.

The bride and groom will choose any music they want played during the ceremony, including hymns for a church service. On the subject of hymn choices this is where most couples aim not to be too original because they want hymns that the guests recognise and can therefore make a decent attempt at singing along to, particularly if there is no choir to guide them. Wedding readings will also be selected, which can include non-religious readings in Church of England ceremonies. The couple will then decide which of their family and/or friends they would like to give the readings, and for a church service they will need to confirm whether there will be bellringers, a choir and/or organist available, and what the Order of Service will be.

LEGAL FORMALITIES

Marriage ceremonies must be overseen by a person authorised to register marriages, and therefore if the couple are having a civil ceremony other than at a register office they must ensure the Superintendent Registrar (Registrar in Northern Ireland) or his/her deputy is available to attend the ceremony. Prior to the ceremony, the couple will meet with the Superintendent Registrar to give notice of their intention to get married and provide certain documents, such as proof of identity. The Superintendent Registrar can then issue authority for them to have a civil wedding at either a register office or an approved premises.

If the couple are having a Church of England wedding they will meet with the vicar to discuss their wedding plans and to provide certain documents. Although it may sometimes be necessary to obtain a licence to allow the marriage to take place, the most common method in the Church of England is to have Banns (an ancient legal tradition dating back to the thirteenth century) read out in church for three Sundays prior to the wedding ceremony, which announces the couple's intention to marry. This also avoids the need to go to the Superintendent Registrar before the wedding. Having done this, the couple can then be married by the vicar on the day of the ceremony.

WEDDING PARTY AND GUESTS

Having chosen the ceremony, reception venue and date, the couple can then decide who, in addition to their parents, will make up the wedding party (also called the bridal party). The groom will make his choice of best man and the bride will decide on her chief bridesmaid. In the same way that you play the key support role for the groom, the chief bridesmaid will perform the same role for the bride. The groom will then decide who the ushers will be, while the bride chooses the other bridesmaids, although they will no doubt discuss their proposals with each other before making the final decisions. They will also decide whether to have any page boys and/or flower girls. It is usual for any siblings of the bride and groom to have roles in the wedding party, together with any children the couple may already have. They may also choose close friends and other family members as bridesmaids and ushers. In fact the bride and groom can have as many of these as they like so long as they feel that the numbers are manageable. Of course there is an expense to consider, not least the special attire to be purchased or hired, although sometimes the bridesmaids/ushers and best man will pay for this themselves.

Once the wedding party roles have been filled, the couple can move on to the guest list. This will start with family and close friends and build up from there. The exact size of the wedding depends mainly on a combination of how many people the couple want to invite, the budget available and the size of the venue chosen. This usually involves a discussion with both sets of parents, particularly if they are contributing to the cost of the wedding.

The couple may also want to invite additional people to attend just the evening party and, if so, that list of guests needs to be drawn up as well.

ENGAGEMENT PARTY AND OTHER GATHERINGS

The couple may arrange a party for family and friends to celebrate their engagement. There is also likely to be a get-together arranged for both sets of parents, particularly if they don't already know each other. This may extend to other members of the wedding party, including the best man.

ATTIRE

Deciding what to wear on the day will probably occupy more of the bride and her attendants' time than the groom and his party. The bride will also be making key decisions about hair styling, make-up and jewellery for the day. For the groom and the other men in the wedding party the decisions are far fewer and much easier, mainly revolving around how formal to be (morning or lounge suits) and remembering to get to the barbers a couple of days ahead of the wedding. It is usual for the men's attire to be hired, and therefore the decision on what to wear needs to be made in plenty of time before the wedding to ensure availability on the day.

RINGS

The couple will purchase their wedding rings (also called wedding bands and usually in platinum or gold), and these are usually given to the best man at some point early on the wedding day ready to be produced during the ceremony. Although it is customary for both the bride and groom to receive a ring, sometimes only one ring is given, from the groom to the bride.

HONEYMOON

Usually the honeymoon is booked by the groom; the couple may take this straight after the wedding, although it is now quite common to delay it until some weeks or months later. The groom may wish to keep the destination as a surprise for the bride. In this case he may want to discuss his honeymoon plans with someone else, but it would probably be better to do this with a female friend rather than his best man. This would avoid, for instance, the groom being forced to explain on arrival how the resort's two golf courses compensates for the absence of a spa complex.

STAG AND HEN PARTIES

While the best man is busy organising the stag party the chief bridesmaid will be arranging the hen party, so it's a good idea for the two of you to keep in touch. For instance, if the bride and groom want both parties on the same day you will need to know what the hen party will be doing. This ensures you don't meet up, unless that is the plan. Although it's usual to have separate stag and hen parties, the bride and groom might decide to break with tradition and have a combined one, or perhaps do the daytime activity together or maybe meet up later in the evening.

OTHER PREPARATIONS FOR THE DAY

Catering and cake

Having decided on the location and number of guests, the couple can start planning the catering. This involves selecting a caterer (if catering isn't already provided by the venue), then reviewing menus and deciding on the drinks to be served (including wine for the meal and something sparkling for the toasts). The wedding cake also needs to be chosen. All these decisions involve a lot of sampling of food and drink, so at this point you might decide it's time to get more actively involved and offer up your services.

The couple will also need to decide whether the budget runs to having a free bar for the evening event. Let's hope so, because as you will have to stay sober until after your speech, you will have a lot of catching up to do!

Recording the day

Once the date is known, the couple can decide on the professional photographer to use and whether they want a videographer for the day. This will involve meeting potential photographers/videographers and reviewing their work and endorsements from previous clients.

For a more personal recording of the day the couple might also choose to place disposable cameras on each of the reception tables for guests to take their own photographs. Another option is to hire a photo booth to help keep the guests entertained and provide them and the bride and groom with another souvenir of the day.

Entertainment

There is a whole variety of entertainment options. Almost certainly for the evening function there will be either a live band or a DJ with mobile disco. The live music can range from solo singers to large bands. Usually these acts will perform cover versions of well-known songs or they may even be a specific tribute band. As an alternative, Jazz and Swing bands are also popular. The couple will want to listen to recordings of any possible bands and may even go and see them live before booking them; the best man could well be invited along to give his opinion. Once booked, the couple can then agree the playlist with the band or DJ, including deciding on the all-important first dance song.

The couple will also decide whether to have any entertainment for the afternoon – for instance, live music such as a harpist, pianist or string quartet is often played during the drinks reception. Other ways to keep guests amused during the day and evening include magicians, caricature artists, fun casinos, living statues, bouncy castles or even fairground rides, such as dodgems, carousels or helter-skelters. If a large number of children will be attending the wedding, one option would be to arrange for a children's entertainer to keep them amused, and to really make their day, the couple could consider hiring an ice-cream van as well.

At the end of the evening the wedding celebrations might be finished off with a fireworks display. As one of the best man's duties is helping to ensure that the day goes smoothly, then the more activities there are, the busier you will be.

Flowers

Leading up to the wedding day the bride, with the help of others, will have chosen a florist and made decisions regarding, most importantly, her bouquet, but also the flowers for the bridesmaids, ceremony location, reception venue and the buttonholes for the men of the wedding party.

Wedding cars and guest transport

The transport to get the bride and her father, plus the mother of the bride and the bridesmaids, to the ceremony will be booked. This will also be used after the ceremony to take the bride and groom to the reception if this is to be held at a different location. There is a great variety of special transport on offer, ranging from vintage Bentleys to horse-drawn carriages. Shuttle transport may be arranged to get the guests from the ceremony to the reception and from the reception back to their hotels at the end of the evening.

Wedding gifts

The couple will almost certainly put together a wedding gift list, which may be held at a particular department store. Often the gift list (or details as to where it is being held) is sent out with the wedding invitations, although some couples may feel a bit uncomfortable doing this. In this case another option is to give details on the couple's wedding website, if they have one set up. Instead of a gift list they may ask for vouchers, contributions to a honeymoon fund or even donations to charity.

The bride will buy gifts for the bridesmaids and the groom will purchase them for his best man and the ushers. Also, the couple will jointly buy gifts for any page boys and/or flower girls.

Wedding invitations and other stationery

The invitations will be ordered, together with any other stationery requirements such as place cards, thank-you cards and Order of Service sheets. Invitations are traditionally sent out by the mother of the bride and usually two to three months before the wedding. Maps and details of possible accommodation in the local area are often included with the invitations, or, as with the gift list, this information could be provided on a wedding website instead.

Seating plan

Once the invitees have RSVP'd and final guest numbers are known, the bride and groom will start to prepare a seating plan for the reception meal. This can be quite a tricky process and it is unlikely to be finished at the first attempt. In fact it's like one of those puzzles you get at Christmas where you try every combination and each time you think the solution is close you realise the last piece doesn't quite fit!

There will usually be a top table where members of the wedding party will sit, with the bride and groom at the centre. Any arrangement of the rest of the wedding party around them is fine, but a typical seating along the table would be as follows: best man, groom's mother, bride's father, bride, groom, bride's mother, groom's father, chief bridesmaid.

(Deciding on an appropriate seating plan if any of the parents of the couple have since remarried can sometimes prove challenging!) The ushers and other bridesmaids would then sit at one of the tables nearest the top table.

Reception room decorations
The bride and groom will have a number of decisions to make regarding the decoration of the reception room, such as choosing chair covers, table decorations including the centrepieces, and deciding on any special lighting requirements. They may also choose to give wedding favours to their guests. By the time they get to making these decisions the groom may well be starting to flag a bit so you will need to be especially attentive, giving him the required encouragement to keep going as the end is near.

The rehearsal
If the couple are having a church wedding the vicar will usually arrange for a rehearsal, either the day before the ceremony or some other time in the week leading up to it, which members of the wedding party will normally attend. Having a run-through of the ceremony ensures that everyone knows exactly what he/she has to do on the day, which will hopefully ensure that everything goes smoothly.

The eve of the wedding
The bride and groom might stay with tradition and not see each other the night before the wedding, in which case the

groom might spend it having a meal with his family and the best man. Alternatively they may decide to have a 'rehearsal dinner', which is an informal get-together of the wedding party and other close family members for a meal. This is a US tradition that is now becoming popular in the UK as well.

2.4 ON THE WEDDING DAY

BEFORE THE CEREMONY
The groom should arrive at the ceremony venue some time before the scheduled start to allow himself and the best man enough time to make sure everything is in order. Accompanied by her father or a relative or friend, the bride will be the last to arrive (for simplicity I have referred to this person as her father in future sections).

CHURCH OF ENGLAND CEREMONY
Guests usually begin arriving at the church up to one hour before the ceremony and it is the responsibility of the ushers to guide them to their seats and hand out the Order of Service sheets. In the church as you look down towards the altar traditionally the family and friends of the bride will be seated on the left and those of the groom will be on the right. Close family members will be seated nearest the front. The groom and best man stand by the front right-hand pew, with the groom on the left and the best man to his right. Traditionally the bride's mother is the last to be seated, escorted by one of the ushers. The bride will enter accompanied by, and holding

the right arm of, her father with the bridesmaids following behind them. As the processional music starts, the party makes its way down the aisle and the groom will turn to greet his bride. The bridesmaids usually follow the bride down the aisle but it's now quite common for them to come down the aisle first. The bride makes her way to the front of the church and stands to the left of her groom.

The Church of England has three possible marriage services: a traditional one from the Book of Common Prayer, a modified version of this, and the Common Worship Service, which is written in modern language. The Common Worship Service proceeds as follows. The vicar begins by welcoming everyone and a hymn may be sung, followed by an introductory statement about marriage. After this the vicar will begin the declarations by asking if anyone present knows of any reason why the couple should not be wed. After a slightly tense silence the bride and groom are also asked to state if they know of any reason why they should not be married and then to declare that they will love, comfort, honour, protect and be faithful to each other. A prayer will then be said, followed by one or more readings (a poem may also be included). There will then be a sermon by the vicar, which may be followed by a second hymn.

Next, the wedding vows will be made between the couple while they hold each other's right hand (this is the part that begins with 'I, [groom's name], take you, [bride's name], to be my wife'). After the vows have been said, the couple will exchange rings. The vicar will then proclaim that the couple are now husband and wife, at which point the newlyweds will kiss and the guests usually applaud and cheer. The vicar will then bless the marriage. A third hymn may be sung or other music played while the couple go into the vestry or side chapel to sign the register. The register is signed by the bride and groom, the vicar, and by two witnesses, usually from the wedding party. Often the chief bridesmaid and the best man act as witnesses, but these could be the fathers of the bride and groom.

Signing the register is a legal requirement, after which the newlyweds will receive a copy of the marriage certificate. The vicar then says the final prayers to end the ceremony. Afterwards the happy couple leave the church, followed by the wedding party, to an appropriately rousing musical accompaniment. Usually the order is the bride and groom, the chief bridesmaid accompanied by the best man, the ushers and bridesmaids, the groom's father and bride's mother and finally the bride's father and groom's mother. The whole ceremony normally lasts up to forty-five minutes depending on the number of hymns and readings.

CIVIL CEREMONY

As previously mentioned, civil marriages take place either at a register office or at an approved premises. Although no religious content is allowed during the ceremony, often the couple will follow the traditional church format with the bride walking down an aisle with attendant bridesmaids to meet the groom, who will be waiting at the front of the venue with his best man.

The ceremony includes a statement about marriage made by the Superintendent Registrar and a declaration whereby the couple state that they know of no reason why they should not be married. They will then say their wedding vows and, although not strictly necessary, rings will often be exchanged, after which the newlyweds will kiss. As with the church service, this is usually accompanied by a round of applause and cheering from the guests. The ceremony only takes about ten to fifteen minutes and afterwards the register is signed by the couple, two witnesses (who do not necessarily need to be known to the couple), the Superintendent Registrar and the Registrar. However, the couple usually have the opportunity to personalise the ceremony by adding readings, poems, music and their own additional vows if they so wish. As register offices may have many bookings there is usually more flexibility to do this if the ceremony takes place at an approved premises. Generally, approved premises also have the advantage of being able to accommodate more guests.

THE RECEPTION

If the ceremony has taken place at a church or register office often the bride and groom will have some of the official photographs taken there before moving on to the reception venue for more photographs and a drinks reception. If the ceremony and reception are at the same location, drinks will normally be served immediately after the ceremony while the main wedding photographs are taken.

The formal part of the reception often begins with the bride and groom, together with their parents (and sometimes the best man, bridesmaids and ushers as well), forming a receiving line at the entrance to where the sit-down meal or buffet will take place. Guests will pass along this line and this is an opportunity for members of the wedding party to greet the guests and for the guests to pass on their best wishes to the bride and groom.

After this the guests will check the seating plan and take their places for the meal, which, given the time of day, is somewhat surprisingly called the wedding breakfast. Usually there will be a top table where the members of the wedding party will sit, with the bride and groom at the centre (*see also* page 76).

The speeches usually begin after the meal, but some couples are now choosing to have them before it, mainly so that the speakers can then relax and enjoy the meal a bit more. Traditionally the custom is for the father of the bride to speak first, followed by the groom and finally the best man. As well as these three traditional speeches, occasionally the bride and/or the chief bridesmaid will also give a speech.

The father of the bride welcomes everyone, particularly the groom's parents, and will then talk about his daughter. He will also welcome his new son-in-law into the family. Following this, he may then have a few words of wisdom about marriage to pass on and will finish with a toast to the bride and groom. The groom will then reply. His speech has a number of purposes, one of which is to thank people on behalf of himself and his wife (i.e. guests, parents, best man, ushers and bridesmaids). He will almost certainly thank his parents for their support during his life up to this point. As well as complimenting his new wife, he may also give one or two anecdotes relating to their relationship, such as how they met. He will then usually present flowers to his mother and the mother of the bride, gifts to the best man, ushers and the bridesmaids before finishing off with a toast to the bridesmaids. Then it's the best man's turn to reply on behalf of the bridesmaids, more of which later. After the best man's speech there will be a short break while he gets a well-earned beer and the guests get over the shock! Then the bride and groom will cut the cake, although this can take place before the speeches. Once everyone has had their cake the main reception ends and there is usually a lull in proceedings while the bride and groom circulate and the best man gets another beer before the evening party starts.

The evening party begins with a first dance by the bride and groom to a romantic song previously chosen by them. As everyone will be watching, they will no doubt have practised this or even taken a few dance lessons. The party continues until the bride and groom leave, often in the early hours of the morning.

Before leaving, the bride will probably throw her bouquet, although she may have done this earlier in the day. The single women will try to catch the bouquet and tradition states that whoever catches it will be the next to marry. As they leave the party the bride and groom will be given a big send-off.

3. THE BEST MAN'S DUTIES BEFORE THE WEDDING DAY

3.1 INTRODUCTION

Having read through the previous chapter you will now have a good idea of all the different activities taking place in the build-up to the wedding and on the day itself. Even though many grooms are increasingly involved in the planning, generally it's still the bride who takes the lead in organising the wedding. This doesn't relieve the groom of his responsibilities though, as the bride will expect him to be actively involved in all the key decisions – other than choosing the wedding dress itself, of course. In addition, the groom usually takes the lead in booking the honeymoon, choosing the ushers and deciding on the attire for the men of the wedding party. So as well as your specific duties you will be providing him with general support and advice on matters relating to the wedding as they come up, which may relate to any of the areas mentioned in Chapter 2.

3.2 THE STAG PARTY

Organising the stag party is your key responsibility prior to the wedding day, and because of the many options available and the amount of administration involved, the whole of the next chapter is devoted to this. The stag party also provides a good opportunity to acquire some anecdotes about the groom's past from his friends for possible inclusion in your speech.

3.3 PREPARING THE SPEECH

Writing the speech is your other main activity prior to the wedding. Once prepared, you will then need to spend some time practising it to help perfect your delivery. Tips and ideas on all areas of preparing and delivering your speech are given in Chapters 6 to 8.

3.4 ATTENDING GATHERINGS

The couple may have a formal engagement party and it's likely that there will be one or two gatherings of close relatives before the wedding. Attending any functions prior to the wedding is important so you get to know who's who in the wedding party, particularly as you might not have met the bride's family previously. In fact you may not know the groom's family that well either, perhaps because you met him at university or work.

Knowing as many guests as possible in advance will help you with the organisation on the wedding day itself. For example, if you are trying to get the bride's family together for the wedding photographs it is useful to be able to identify whom you are looking for without having to ask.

These events also provide an opportunity to meet any of the ushers you don't already know, which is useful since you will be directing them in their duties on the day. They in turn will be able to meet those members of the wedding party whom they themselves don't already know. Treat such gatherings as research opportunities for the speech as well. This is especially helpful if you didn't grow up with the groom, because you should be able to find out stories about him from when he was a child, which could provide some good material. Even the bride may be willing to divulge some amusing, if not too personal, details about their relationship (romantic and not so romantic moments). Make sure you clear anything you will be using from these conversations in your speech with her first, though.

In addition to these more formal meetings of key family members you will almost certainly meet with the bride, groom and chief bridesmaid on a regular basis to discuss wedding matters. As the chief bridesmaid will probably also be very busy with preparations, you will have a kindred spirit to discuss and compare notes with – for example, relating to the administration of the stag and hen parties.

3.5 OTHER DUTIES

USHERS

The groom will usually ask the best man for his opinion on the choice of ushers, particularly as you will be co-ordinating them on the day, so you need to be confident that they are reliable individuals who will perform their duties well. Ideally there should be at least one usher from the bride's side and one from the groom's so that they can identify as many of the guests as possible. As well as ensuring guests are greeted by a familiar face on arrival at the wedding ceremony, this also helps throughout the day – for example, when it comes to gathering groups for the photographs.

ATTIRE

The best man also helps the groom to decide what the men in the wedding party will be wearing on the day. Usually he will choose matching morning or lounge suits with accompanying waistcoats, pocket handkerchiefs, cravats or ties (with morning suits, possibly top hats as well). An alternative, particularly if the wedding is to be held later in the day, would be to go for black tie (dinner jacket with bow tie and cummerbund). The colour and style of whatever formal wear is chosen needs to co-ordinate with the general theme of the wedding. For example, the colour for the cravats shouldn't clash with the bridesmaids' dresses. One way for the groom to stand out from the rest of the men in the wedding party is for him to choose a different coloured or designed waistcoat.

The best man accompanies the groom to any required fittings, which ideally the ushers should attend as well. If you are hiring formal wear, check what is included and whether there are any items that you will need to provide yourself, such as a shirt, shoes or cufflinks.

ACCOMMODATION

The groom and the best man will normally stay at the same place the night before the wedding, so if the wedding is not taking place in your hometown then you will need to ensure that accommodation for yourself and the groom has been booked. At the same time, make sure that you have your own accommodation arranged for the wedding night.

WEDDING PRESENTS

Your present for the bride and groom can either come from their wedding gift list or as best man you may decide to choose something slightly more personal. If you are buying from the wedding gift list, do this sooner rather than later so that you have a good selection of ideas to choose from.

CAR DECORATIONS

If you and the ushers plan to decorate the going-away car, make sure you have bought the relevant items such as cans, string, shaving cream and a 'Just Married' sign in plenty of time. Also, make sure that whatever you use will not damage the car paint.

3.6 THE REHEARSAL

If the wedding is to take place in a church then it's quite likely that there will be a rehearsal sometime during the week before, which you will usually attend. Again, this is a great opportunity to get to know people and you will gain a better understanding of what you need to do during the ceremony. It's a good idea to listen to what the groom has to do as well, so that if he forgets, you will be able to remind him on the day.

Attending the rehearsal allows you to see the venue to ensure you understand exactly how the seating will be arranged. If it's a civil ceremony and no rehearsal is planned, it's a good idea to arrange with the manager of the venue a convenient time when you can visit to familiarise yourself with the layout. You will also need to check with the groom whether there are any particular seating requirements, such as following the church norm of having the bride's family and friends on the left and the groom's on the right. While you are at the church or civil ceremony venue, you should make sure that there is adequate parking and, if not, what the overspill arrangements will be. This information will then need to be communicated to the ushers.

3.7 THE ITINERARY

You will be helping with the general organisation on the wedding day and making sure everything runs on time. To do this effectively, familiarise yourself with the itinerary for the day, which the groom should be able to provide. This should give the key activities taking place and the approximate timings, such as the start time for the ceremony, when the bride and groom need to leave for the reception, what time the meal is due to begin, and when the transport is booked for the end of the evening. As the happy couple will be preoccupied with everything else going on during the day they will almost certainly be unaware of how quickly time is passing, so you will need to do the timekeeping for them.

3.8 THE EVE OF THE WEDDING

There will undoubtedly be a bit of last-minute running around on the day before the wedding. You should therefore be prepared to help out as and when required. One job you will need to do is to collect any hired clothes for yourself and the groom. It's a good idea for you both to try them on one last time just to make sure the fitting is correct. Usually the ushers will collect their own hired clothes, but you should check this with them.

Make sure you know the arrangements for buttonholes for yourself and the groom in the morning (usually they will be delivered to you, or you will pick them up from the bride's parents' home). If it's a church ceremony, make sure the ushers have the Order of Service sheets in plenty of time before the ceremony. It's worth speaking to the ushers sometime during the day to confirm these and other wedding-day arrangements.

If there are some guests who cannot make the wedding they may have sent emails or cards, so you will need to collect these (probably from the mother of the bride) as you will be reading them out during your speech.

The best man is responsible for getting the groom to the ceremony. No special transport is required so your own car is fine so long as it's roadworthy and reliable. If you are driving, consider taking your car to the carwash during the day so that it looks its best when you arrive at the ceremony. Also, make sure you have a back-up plan if the car doesn't start in the morning, such as having the number of a local taxi firm. In addition, map out an alternative route in case there are problems on the roads. If you are taking a taxi, it's a good idea to call in the evening to confirm the pick-up time.

Connected with being prepared for last-minute hiccups, don't forget to charge your mobile phone and add to your contact list the phone numbers of key family members in case you need to get in touch with them before the ceremony.

Find a quiet moment sometime during the day for one final run-through of your speech.

As you and the groom need to be at your best on the wedding day you will probably have a reasonably quiet evening, maybe with the groom's close family. However, if a larger event has been organised, you will have to take charge here to ensure the groom doesn't have too late a night; you will be blamed if he arrives looking tired and hungover for the ceremony.

One final thing to remember is to set the alarm, particularly if it's a morning ceremony. When setting it, make sure that you allow for the extra time needed for getting ready in the morning.

3.9 CHECKLIST

ACTIVITIES BEFORE THE WEDDING DAY

Activity	Timing	Completed
Key dates in diary, including family gatherings and rehearsal	ASAP	
Stag party arranged (see Chapter 4 for detailed checklist)	ASAP	
Speech prepared	ASAP	
Accommodation booked	ASAP	
Help choose the ushers, if asked	As required	

Activity	Timing	Completed
Suit fittings attended	As required	
Wedding present bought	1–2 months before	
Going-away car decorations purchased	Week before	
Itinerary for the wedding day obtained and reviewed	Week before	
Taxi to ceremony booked, if applicable	Week before	
Rehearsal attended or venue visited	Week before	
Key mobile numbers obtained and phone charged	Wedding eve	
Taxi to ceremony re-confirmed or car checked and washed	Wedding eve	
Formal wear collected, if hired. Check you have all items not hired (e.g. cufflinks, shoes)	Wedding eve	
Emails/cards from absent friends collected	Wedding eve	
Spoken to ushers and confirmed arrangements (e.g. for collecting the Order of Service sheets)	Wedding eve	
Arrangements for the buttonholes confirmed	Wedding eve	
Speech and props with you	Wedding eve	
Alarm set	Wedding eve	

4. THE STAG PARTY

4.1 INTRODUCTION

I expect that you may have been on a few stag dos before and so you already have a general idea of what is required to arrange one. This will help but it's always different when you are the one organising the event, not least having the extra pressure of being responsible for its success. To ensure that you arrange the best possible stag party for your groom you will need to have considered all the possible options available. These can range from an evening in the pub to a full weekend abroad with activities. Having decided on what to do, when to do it and whom to invite, you will then be responsible for organising the event. This includes communicating with everyone involved, making bookings, collecting money, making payments and then making sure everything goes to plan on the day/weekend itself. This chapter will guide you through the whole process.

4.2 SURPRISE THE GROOM

The groom will need to be involved in deciding when to hold the stag party and also who should be on the list of invitees. It's then up to you both to decide whether he's also involved in choosing what to do. There's an added excitement to the proceedings when the groom doesn't know where he's going, or what he will be doing. On the downside there is more pressure on you to choose something he will enjoy. Still, as you know him well, and with suggestions from the rest of the group, you should be able to put together a stag do he will remember, in a good way.

If you are not involving the groom in the planning, you might like to choose someone else in the group to be your right-hand man to help with the organisation and discuss ideas with.

Rather than making the stag do a complete surprise and risk disappointing the groom, you could get a few ideas of what he would like to do and then make the final selection based on this shortlist. If you do this he will still be in the dark regarding the exact itinerary planned and you can keep the evening entertainment as a surprise.

4.3 TIMING

As everyone needs time to recover, you rarely hear of the stag party being held the night before the wedding anymore, except perhaps in films. Usually it's held around a month before the wedding day. The exact date chosen will be a combination of what suits the groom and when a majority of the invitees are available. If the hen party is to be held at the same time then the date also needs to suit the bride and her party. The flexibility regarding dates will be more limited, the more complex the stag party planned. For example, arranging an overseas trip requires the availability of flights, accommodation and activities, so this needs to be planned as far in advance as possible.

4.4 INVITEES

The groom will probably have a good idea whom he wants to invite on his stag do. Usually he will invite any brothers he has and all his male friends who are attending the wedding. He will probably extend the invitation to any brothers of the bride. In most cases only people over eighteen years old are invited. Occasionally the fathers of the bride and groom will be invited, although this is unusual and they wouldn't normally expect to receive an invitation. How much further the groom extends the invitation depends partly on numbers and how well he knows the people involved – there are no formal rules.

Once you have the final list of invitees you should get their email addresses from the groom so you are ready to contact them regarding the details of the event. Alternatively, you could set up a Facebook group to keep in touch.

4.5 WHAT MAKES A GREAT STAG PARTY?

As the best man you are responsible for organising a great event, but don't feel that it needs to be on a grand scale to be successful. Some of the best stag parties are small affairs just held locally during the course of an evening. Doing lots of activities or travelling overseas can add to the experience and memorability, but the real success of a stag do is more about creating the right sort of atmosphere so that everyone is in the mood to have a good time.

There may be more than one group of the groom's friends drawn together for the stag party, perhaps from school, university, work or a sports club, together with one or two relatives. Some people, for example old school friends, may not have caught up in a while and so they will want to chat, but you need to ensure there is some way of bringing everyone together as a group early on. This will be easier if the stag party begins with an afternoon activity, especially if it's a team event. If not, you will probably want to meet in a pub or bar, even if it's just at the airport, as a couple of early drinks will help break the ice. You could combine this with a quiz about the groom, which allows you to group people in teams from different parts of his life. This makes sense as it enables each team to answer a wider range of questions and immediately mixes the group up. If you do this in a bar you could also add a drinking forfeit element.

To help people remember who's who you could get some ID tags made up for everyone to wear. In addition to having names on them, they could also include some amusing personal information and how each of them is connected to the groom. This should help get the conversation going between the stags (and probably with other people in the bar as well!). Whatever you decide to do, once everyone has got to know each other the stag party should be carried along by its own momentum, not least due to the amount of alcohol being consumed.

4.6 WHAT TO DO

INTRODUCTION
Before making detailed decisions about what to do, you will need to establish the scale of the event that the groom would

like you to organise. So does he want just an evening do, a day/evening event with activities, or a full weekend away? And before making this decision you will almost certainly need to consider what the rough cost of each option would be, particularly if you are thinking of having an overseas stag party. A lot of destinations are reasonably cheap to get to on low-cost airlines, but people have different budgets. When making estimates it's best to err on the side of caution because it's easy to underestimate what the actual cost will be when you have flights, taxis, accommodation, daytime activities, clubs, as well as meals and drinks to take into account. Having made your rough cost estimate, you can then check with the groom whether this would prevent some people from attending. If so, it may be better to hold a smaller event closer to home. Remember when preparing cost estimates you will probably want to divide the groom's costs for any activities and the evening out among yourself and the other stags as it's traditional for these to be covered by everyone else.

Another factor to consider before deciding on the complexity of the event is how many people you expect to attend. Generally the more people who will be going, the simpler you will want to make the stag do to keep it manageable, so if you plan on going overseas you will almost certainly want a smaller group than if you were going to go out locally.

Having decided on the scale of the stag party, the key objective then is to find something to do that your groom will enjoy. So if he has always dreamed of a stag weekend diving in a shark cage off the coast of South Africa then it's your job to see that he changes his mind, otherwise he will probably be spending it on his own! Although your main priority is to arrange a stag party the groom will enjoy, you also need to consider what the other stags might like to do as well. Of course you want the stag party to be as original as possible but you may not want to be too adventurous as you will probably have quite a mix of people going, with different likes and dislikes. So, although you may not be able to please everyone, you need to choose something that the majority will enjoy. As mentioned earlier, if the groom is not involved in the preparations it would be useful to have someone else to work through different ideas with. You may then decide to circulate your top two or three proposals around the group, together with cost estimates and make the final choice based on the majority view.

In the remainder of this section you will find suggestions for daytime activities, ideas for what to do in the evening, what to consider if you are planning a weekend away and details of some of the most popular UK and overseas destinations for stag parties.

DAYTIME ACTIVITY OPTIONS
There is a wide variety of possible activities to consider when deciding what to do during the day. If you are holding the stag party locally you will be limited by what activities are available within a reasonable driving distance of home. When arranging a weekend away, the choice of location may be influenced by what there is to do in or around the town or

city you will be visiting. The more popular activities such as paintballing and go-karting are available nationally and in most overseas locations as well, but for some activities your location options will be more restricted.

Of course there is no need to do anything organised or active on the stag do. If you are visiting somewhere new, particularly overseas, you might just choose to look round the city, and, if it's a lively place such as Barcelona, simply soak up the atmosphere or head for the beach. However, if you are not doing an organised activity it's probably a good idea to avoid the temptation of sitting in a bar drinking all day; you will need to pace yourselves as you have a big night out later on. On the other hand, if you can't resist a daytime drink, consider doing something a bit different and combine drinking with sightseeing and some exercise by taking a beer bike tour, which is available in quite a few European cities.

To give you an idea of the types of activities that are available, I have listed a selection of them below. When choosing what to do, bear in mind that the cost of doing different activities can vary significantly. If you want to do more than one activity, consider going to an activity centre, most of which will offer half-day or full-day multi-activity packages for stag parties. In the appendix of stag party online resources (see page 149), you will find details of some of these centres, together with other activity providers and organisations.

General sports and activities – abseiling, archery, blow karting, canyoning, caving, five-a-side football, golf, high ropes, horse riding, it's a knockout, laser games, mountain biking, paintballing, rock climbing, shooting (clay pigeon or target), skydiving, tenpin bowling and zorbing.

Motorsports – buggies (for example, rage, power turn), go-karting, hovercrafting, quad biking and other driving experiences (off-road, stock car, sports car, tank, JCB, rally).

Watersports – canoeing, coasteering, deep-sea fishing, jet-skiing, kitesurfing, power boating, sailing, scuba diving, surfing, wake boarding, waterskiing, white-water rafting, windsurfing and Zapcats.

Winter sports – bobsleighing, skiing, snowboarding and snow mobiles.

Spectator sports – cricket, football, greyhounds, horse racing and rugby.

Non-active – Brewery and distillery tours, theme parks and wine tasting.

When deciding what activity to choose, it's a good idea to have a back-up plan in case it is cancelled at the last minute due to some reason beyond your control. In the case of one stag do that I attended, the plan was to watch horse racing at Sedgefield, but on the day itself the race meeting was called off. Instead we headed for the coast to watch Hartlepool at home to Rotherham. Yes, I know – we were surprised that there were still tickets available on the morning of the match too! Even though it was a while back, I still remember that game, not for the score (none of us was a fan of either club) but for just how bitterly cold it was as we were pounded for ninety minutes by freezing winds whipping off the North Sea, and this was in April. You can only admire the endurance of Hartlepool fans.

If you are planning a full weekend stag party, you might decide to arrange a formal activity for the Sunday as well. You will need to take into account that everyone will be a bit tired and probably hungover as well, so you won't want to do anything too early in the day or too demanding. A round of golf is therefore preferable to white-water rafting. The alternative is maybe to have a late breakfast, and, if you are visiting somewhere new, just take a look around and do some sightseeing or even, dare I say it, do something cultural such as visit a museum or gallery. If you go the cultural route then it's worth keeping it to yourselves; if the bride hears about it, she will definitely be suspicious that you are all hiding something! Alternatively, you may wish to stay at a hotel with a leisure centre or spa and use the facilities since it's a good way to relax on the day after the main event.

If you want to do something a bit different you could hire a canal boat for the weekend. The UK has an extensive network of waterways to choose from so you shouldn't have to travel too far to do this (see Appendix, page 150). Another option would be to plan the stag party to coincide with a particular festival. As well as the larger, well-known festivals there are many others going on throughout the year in the UK and the rest of Europe, which could add an extra focus to a weekend away. Amsterdam alone has over ninety festivals taking place during the year.

EVENING ENTERTAINMENT OPTIONS

The traditional stag party evening begins with a few drinks either in one pub or as part of a pub crawl. If you do this then it's worth having a few drinking games ready as they are good group activities and will add a bit of variety to the proceedings. At some point in the evening the serious drinking is usually interrupted while everyone goes to a restaurant for a meal. Often the event is finished off with a trip to a nightclub.

Although drinking usually features heavily in whatever is planned, there are a few alternatives to this. For example you might consider combining drinking with sightseeing and book a riverboat booze cruise or maybe hire a party bus. Alternatively, you may decide to visit a casino, although with the amount of alcohol being consumed you will need to ensure that no one ends up losing his shirt! Other options are to visit a comedy club or live music venue, or perhaps spend the early evening either at a greyhound track or watching some horse racing.

Some stag parties will include a trip to a lap-dancing club, which has generally replaced hiring a stripper as the adult entertainment option. People have different views on the acceptability of this form of entertainment, so even if you think the groom will enjoy the experience, you should discuss it with him first as he will know the views of the other stags in your party – and more importantly what the bride's reaction is likely to be if she finds out!

WEEKEND LOCATIONS

Introduction

Stag weekends are usually great fun. There's nothing like going away with 'the lads', bonding over group activities, drinking lots of beer and exploring a new city, while giving the groom a good send-off. This probably explains why they have become so popular in recent years, and every year more new cities are being explored by adventurous stag parties and added to the pool of possible destinations. In some ways this does make your job even harder, though, as there are now so many places to choose from. Hopefully, this section will give you some ideas to help you in your search for the ideal weekend location for your own stag party. Before discussing specific UK and overseas destinations there are a few general points to consider regarding the location and accommodation choices.

It's probably fair to say that stag parties are not necessarily a city's ideal weekend tourists, but as you will be spending a reasonable amount of cash, it's not all bad news for the local businesses. But it's certainly worth investigating if some places might be more welcoming than others. This will change from year to year, since a city which has been popular and welcoming over a number of years might now have become a bit tired of endless stag parties roaming the streets.

You may decide to go to a less popular destination to avoid being just one of many stag parties out on the town or in the city centre on a Saturday night. Certainly some of the smaller locations will quickly feel saturated with only a few stag parties out and about in the evening. Cornwall's Newquay is a prime example of a small town that is now very popular with stag parties, although they may not stand out so much there since the local council banned offensive T-shirts and inflatables in June 2011. On the plus side, if a town is popular with stag parties, it will be set up to cater for them (and of course it will also be popular with hen parties). However, if you choose somewhere a bit different, not only will you have the novelty factor and the locals might be more welcoming, but as none of the stags may have previously visited there for a stag party, you will get full marks for originality.

If you want to find out what other people attending stag parties thought of a particular city then you will find comments online – for example on Twitter (www.twitter.com) or on the websites of some of the stag party organisers, such as Chillisauce Experiences (www.chillisauce.co.uk).

Also, wherever you go, when you are out and about bear in mind that as a group of blokes who have had a few drinks, you may be slightly more boisterous than you realise. Although you will probably be met by nothing but friendly locals who, like you, are just out to have a good time, remember to show appropriate consideration towards them.

This will prevent any chances of your pub crawl turning into a street brawl.

When going on a stag weekend you will want to make sure that the Saturday night is the main event, so take it easy on the Friday evening, otherwise you may find everyone's energy levels will be drained for the following night. People need to pace themselves, and even if you have been travelling on the Friday, there is still a temptation to hit the ground running once you arrive and then find yourselves too hungover for the rest of the weekend to enjoy it. The alternative, particularly for UK-based stag parties, is to arrive on the Friday or Saturday and just stay one night. This also has the advantage of keeping the costs down, although it may be difficult to find hotels that will accept a one-night booking at the weekend during the peak season.

Accommodation

On a stag do people are generally happy to stay in budget accommodation, particularly as they will have a lot of other costs over the weekend. Although staying in a hotel is the most common option, you might consider booking an apartment, particularly if you will be visiting a summer holiday destination such as one of the Spanish resorts where apartments should be readily available and may work out as the cheaper option.

Although most weekend stag parties base themselves in a town or city, as you may spend at least part of the trip in the surrounding countryside participating in outdoor activities, consider staying in the countryside, perhaps near an activity centre. Options include booking a self-catering holiday cottage, a B&B, or staying at a hostel or on a campsite, and this would certainly bring the costs down. If you plan on visiting an activity centre, some of them have accommodation available onsite and most will be able to provide you with details of suitable places to stay nearby. If you do stay in the countryside you could always arrange transport to and from the local town or city for the Saturday night.

UK locations

If you are staying in the UK you are spoilt for choice with the number of potential locations to hold your stag party. In fact anywhere with a reasonably decent nightlife is a possibility, which is probably why most stag parties are held in or close to the groom's hometown. Even if the local town has an excellent nightlife, the stag party provides a good excuse to venture a bit further afield and try somewhere new. You may decide to choose a place with a particular connection to the groom – for example, where he attended university. If you are thinking of going away for the weekend, current popular choices include Bournemouth, Brighton, Bristol, Cardiff, Edinburgh, Liverpool, London, Newcastle, Newquay and Nottingham.

Together with many other places around the UK, these towns and cities have great evening entertainment on offer, with a good variety of pubs, bars, restaurants and clubs. Each one will have a different feel about it, so although you probably have a good idea as to what to expect in most UK towns and cities, you may want to do a bit of further research before firming up on your final choice to make sure you have considered all the possible options.

To help start your research here are a few reasons why the ten UK locations listed below are popular stag party destinations.

Location	Key features
Bournemouth	Seaside holiday atmosphere, golden sandy beaches, decent weather and great watersports (e.g. windsurfing and jet-skiing).
Brighton	Lives up to its 'London by the sea' tag with a vibrant atmosphere unlike any other seaside town. It's a great place to spend a Sunday relaxing in a cafe after a big night out.
Bristol	Lots of bars surrounding the quayside, so perfect for a pub crawl. Plenty to see and do in the area – for instance, while abseiling in the Avon Gorge, you could be admiring the Clifton Suspension Bridge.
Cardiff	Millennium Stadium for sports fans and other events, re-developed quayside with lively bars, and spectacular countryside for outdoor activities such as rock climbing and canyoning.
Edinburgh	Scotland's capital has a great atmosphere; it is also a cultural centre with lots of sights to see, including the castle. You could also try a distillery tour and a round of golf.
Liverpool	Lively nightlife, with clubs and bars all conveniently close together. Lots to see related to the Beatles, and if you're not too hungover you could take a ferry across the Mersey.
London	Pubs, bars, restaurants, clubs, theatres, live music, sports, sights, the River Thames, markets, galleries, museums … Basically, the capital city has everything for a fantastic stag weekend.

Location	Key features
Newcastle	Attractive city centre and iconic quayside. A great place for a night out, which is why, when you think of stag parties, Newcastle is one of the first places to come to mind.
Newquay	Famous for its party atmosphere and of course the perfect place to try surfing, but there are many other adrenalin-fuelled activities to enjoy as well, such as coasteering.
Nottingham	The city's central location, combined with its variety of pubs, bars and clubs, makes it an ideal stag destination – and if you want to do something relaxing, you could always watch some cricket.

Overseas locations

If you are planning a weekend overseas for the stag party there are obviously many potential locations to choose from. Your choice will almost certainly be influenced by a combination of the overall cost, what there is to see and do during the day, and the evening entertainment on offer.

Places go in and out of fashion for stag weekends and this in part is influenced by where the budget airlines are currently flying and offering good deals to. Most overseas stag weekends tend to be held somewhere in Europe due to the cheap airfares and short travelling times. Such is the variety of locations in Europe that you should find something to suit you without having to look further afield. If not, there is always Las Vegas.

A few years ago Dublin was probably the most popular overseas choice for stag parties, but with the accessibility and low cost of Eastern European locations, these have become increasingly popular. However, many of these countries are not as cheap as they once were so you do need to do some advance research to ensure that you are not unpleasantly surprised by the cost of going out for the evening in whichever city you choose.

Current popular European destinations include Amsterdam, Berlin, Budapest, Dublin, Krakow, Prague and Riga. Many locations in Spain are also popular, such as Barcelona and Ibiza. Each city will have a similar selection of evening entertainment and should offer the more popular daytime activities too. However, the range of daytime activities available will vary significantly between locations. For instance, you could be firing AK-47s in Prague, blow karting near Amsterdam or sailing around Ibiza.

The contrast between the feel of the different cities will of course be far greater than between UK cities. So if you plan on going overseas you will probably want to research a variety of locations to ensure you have chosen the best place for your particular group. For example, you may have a good idea of what to expect in some of the more popular cities such as Amsterdam, but perhaps not in Riga. Your choice of destination may also be influenced by when the stag party is taking place, as the climate in some European cities varies significantly between summer and winter.

Here are a few reasons why the ten overseas locations listed below make popular stag party destinations.

Location	Key features
Amsterdam	Amsterdam has some great clubs and bars, in addition to the evening entertainment for which it's more famous. During the day you can relax by hiring bikes and cycling along the canals between numerous coffee shops.
Barcelona	If it's a sophisticated stag party you want, Barcelona is the place to go, and as well as the bars, cafes and culture of a major city, it also has excellent beaches – and of course the Camp Nou.
Berlin	One of Europe's top club scenes which, when combined with the excellent beer served in its bars, makes Berlin a great stag party location. There are also many interesting places to visit connected to the city's more recent history.
Budapest	A very attractive city with lots to see and do; also the beer is cheap so perfect for a stag party. After a big night out, take a cruise down the Danube or relax in one of the thermal baths.
Dublin	Great atmosphere in the pubs, especially those with traditional live music, so there's no better place for a pub crawl and friendly locals. You could also visit the Guinness Brewery for a Storehouse Tour.
Ibiza	Combine probably the world's most famous clubbing destination with hot sunny weather and the beach, and you have a perfect mix for a stag weekend away.
Krakow	Poland's cultural capital has a historic and attractive old town – a great setting to enjoy the many bars selling cheap beer. If you are visiting in winter, you could go trekking on snowmobiles in the surrounding hills.
Las Vegas	Perhaps the ultimate stag party location. As well as the casinos, hotels, bars, clubs and shows on 'The Strip', you could also take a tour of the Grand Canyon or try skydiving.

Location	Key features
Prague	The city has some beautiful buildings in the old town, overlooked by the castle, and is one of the cultural centres of Europe. This, together with the lively nightlife, makes it a great place to visit.
Riga	Latvia's capital is one of the largest cities in the Baltics with nightlife to match centred round the pretty old town. Riga is extremely cold in winter but the vodka should warm you up and you could always try bobsleighing.

4.7 STAG NIGHT TRADITIONS

LOOKING THE PART

One decision to make as part of the preparations is whether to organise something distinctive for all the stags to wear, a common choice being T-shirts announcing that you are on the groom's stag do. Other accessories you might consider are headgear (antlers, wigs, police helmets, etc.), celebrity masks, fake facial hair, novelty inflatables, and so on. Another option is to have a particular theme (such as James Bond) and to dress accordingly. If you want the groom to stand out from the other members of the stag party, and depending on how embarrassed you want him to be, you could dress him in drag or perhaps a fancy dress outfit. Bear in mind that if you are all wearing something distinctive, this could make gaining entry to some bars and clubs more difficult. Details of some online suppliers of accessories are given in the appendix (page 150).

LAMP-POSTS AND OTHER PRANKS

If you want to maintain the tradition of attaching a partially clothed groom to a lamp-post at some point in the evening, you will find that most online stag party accessory suppliers sell handcuffs and tape. If this seems a bit harsh or predictable, then you might try something else. Any practical joke is fine so long as no one gets physically or mentally damaged (which might rule out a fake kidnapping in some cities). Another popular stag-do tradition is to give the groom a few dares to complete during the evening. These could be anything light-hearted which might embarrass him a bit but at the same time not cause offence to anyone else. Often the dares involve the groom undertaking a challenge in a bar, such as dancing, singing, revealing a secret to a stranger, persuading a girl to buy him a drink, etc.

If the stag party details are to be a surprise for the groom, one harmless prank is to give him the impression that you will be doing something else. For example, if the groom is a big golf fan and you have booked a round at a famous course, you could first take him to a nearby public pitch-and-putt course and pretend you will be playing there. I do know someone who played this trick the other way round but that was perhaps a bit too cruel!

As far as prank props are concerned, the main rule is to avoid anything living. As a word of warning related to this, stags on a stag party in Bournemouth in 2011 ended up in court after putting live chickens in the groom's hotel room; the incriminating evidence showing the arrival and departure of the 'hen party' was caught on the hotel CCTV.

DRINKING GAMES

There are many drinking games but here are three popular ones, although I expect you will have your own favourites. The first two are pretty straightforward and the last one is a bit more involved, but they are all good icebreakers.

Fuzzy duck

One player starts by saying 'fuzzy duck'. The player to his left says either 'fuzzy duck' or 'does he'. If the second player says 'fuzzy duck', then the play passes to the next person round the table. If any player says 'does he', this reverses the play and also the phrase, which would go from 'fuzzy duck' to 'ducky fuzz'. If two players say 'does he' one after the other, play continues in the same direction as before with the same phrase. The round goes on until someone makes a mistake or hesitates for too long and has to take a drink.

The name game

Someone starts by saying the name of a famous person. The next person then names someone famous, whose first name begins with the first letter of the surname of the previous person. For example, Judi Dench – David Cameron – Christopher Columbus (direction change) – Christian Bale – Bono (direction change). Direction changes occur when the first name and the surname start with the same letter or if the person has only one name. Anyone who hesitates for too long or can't think of a name takes a drink.

Ring of fire

Place a pint glass in the middle of the table and spread a pack of playing cards face down around it. Everyone then takes turns in picking up a card. Each card has a meaning. There are many variations but here is one set of rules you could use:

Ace   Everyone keeps drinking until the person who picked up the card stops.

2   You – Choose someone to drink.

3   Me – You drink.

4   Floor – Touch the floor, last person takes a drink.

5   When you put your thumb on the table everyone else follows and the last person takes a drink. You can do this whenever you like until someone else picks a five.

6   Everyone drinks.

7   Heaven – Point your finger skyward and whoever is last takes a drink.

8   Mate – Choose someone else to drink with you.

9   Rhyme – Pick a word and the next person has to find a word that rhymes with it, and so on round the table. Anyone who can't think of a word takes a drink.

10   Categories – Pick a category (for example, Disney movies), and the next person says something related to that category. If they can't think of anything, they take a drink.

Jack   Make a rule (for example, no swearing) and everyone has to follow it for the whole game or take a drink.

Queen Questions – Go round the table with each person asking a question of the next. If someone doesn't ask a question, they take a drink.

King   Pour some of your drink into the beer glass in the middle. Whoever picks up the last King drinks whatever is in the glass.

4.8 LOOK AFTER THE GROOM

As well as making sure that everyone has a good time on the stag do and the groom is on the receiving end of the odd harmless prank, as best man you are responsible for ensuring that he makes it home in one piece. You will also have to keep an eye on everyone else to ensure that anyone who gets a little worse for wear is taken care of. I mentioned the cautionary stag-night tale of the groom who ended up having his jaw sewn up in the introduction to this book but there are many more instances of the groom ending the night not in a club but in a hospital A&E unit instead. As the best man it is down to you to be the voice of reason when after a few drinks the prank ideas become increasingly inventive. If you need to focus your mind on this responsibility, remember you will be the one phoning your friend's fiancée in the morning to explain any mishap. Also, mislaying the groom on a stag do seems as easy as losing your keys, especially if you are doing a pub crawl so make sure you keep an eye on him. Of course this will be easier if he's dressed in a bright yellow banana suit!

4.9 PROFESSIONAL STAG PARTY ORGANISERS

If you have decided to make the stag party a full weekend, this requires considerable organisation and some best men will use the services of specialist stag party organisers. A stag party organiser will take care of most of the administration and this includes making the relevant bookings for hotels and daytime activities (if travelling overseas, it is usually down to you to arrange your own flights). They will also provide assistance in preparing the evening itinerary, including recommendations of bars to visit and arranging entry to clubs. In addition, they will deal with the receipts and payment side of things, including taking deposits and final payments from the stags using some form of online payments system. This service is particularly useful if you are planning an overseas stag party and are unfamiliar with the country. For instance, if you want to book a daytime activity abroad, it may be difficult for you to establish whether the local activity provider is a reputable one.

If you do go for this option, before confirming your booking make sure you are clear as to what is included in the overall cost and what you will need to book separately (for example, does the price include transport to and from daytime activities?). Should you need to make amendments to your booking (maybe someone has dropped out or you simply want to change the itinerary), most organisers will allow you to do this free of charge up until the final payment is due, which is usually around a month before you travel.

One option you might consider is booking part of your trip with a specialist organiser, such as the daytime activity or the entry tickets to a stag-friendly nightclub. Most organisers will do this if you ask.

Ideally you will select an organiser based on personal recommendation, or perhaps you yourself have been on a successful stag party previously organised by them. If not, you should be able to get a reasonable idea as to how good they are going to be from the general helpfulness, knowledge and professionalism of the staff when you first make contact. In addition, prior to booking you may wish to check out some of the online comments from previous customers. If you prefer to book through a larger organisation you can get an idea of the size of the business by looking online at the variety of activities and locations on offer and ask questions such as how many staff they have and how many stag parties they deal with annually. Whoever you book with, it is also worth checking how long they have been in business.

Website details for some stag party organisers are given in the appendix (page 149).

4.10 ADMINISTRATION

This section provides guidance on the key administrative tasks and some of the more general points to consider when organising a stag party. How much of this will be relevant to your specific stag party depends on the scale of the event you are organising and whether or not you are using a professional stag party organiser.

COMMUNICATION

To successfully administer the stag party there needs to be good communication between you and the other stags throughout the process, right from the start when you discuss what to do through to the day before when you remind everyone where to meet. As mentioned earlier, the best method for keeping in touch is either by email or by setting up a Facebook group. You will also need to get everyone's mobile phone numbers for keeping in touch on the stag do itself.

RECEIPTS AND PAYMENTS

If you are arranging everything yourself you will probably make most of the payments on behalf of the group. When collecting money from people it will be easier if they all pay you using the same method. The best way to do this would be for you to provide them with your bank details and they can then pay the money directly into your account. Ask them to add their name as an identifying reference on any transfer they make. If you will be making any payments on behalf of the group, ensure that everyone pays you upfront first, which means setting some tough deadlines. Even if you do this you will probably still have to spend quite a lot of time chasing people for money. Unfortunately this is just one of the hassles of the job.

CANCELLATIONS

You and the other stags will need to have a clear understanding of what happens regarding costs should anyone in the group drop out – for example, cancellation fees, the loss of deposits paid or the cost of tickets purchased. This ensures that there will be no nasty surprises and, most importantly, that you yourself don't end up out of pocket.

BOOKINGS

As a general point it's a good idea to make bookings using a credit card. If there are any subsequent problems and you are unable to claim a refund from the company (perhaps because they have gone out of business), you should be able to get your money back from the credit card issuer (this applies to transactions over £100).

When making bookings, remember to ask for an email confirmation so you have a record of the booking.

TRAVEL, TRANSPORT AND ACCOMMODATION

If you are arranging a weekend stag party you will need to book accommodation and, if travelling abroad, flights too. When booking flights, one way to find the cheapest available is to use flight comparison websites as these will search through most, if not all, of the available flights. There are many of these, of which Skyscanner (www.skyscanner.net) and Kayak (www.kayak.co.uk) are probably the best known. If you select a flight using one of these websites they will usually re-direct you to the airline or travel agent for you to make the booking directly. It's worth checking more than one website, and possibly the airline's own website, to ensure the best possible deal. Many sites have mobile apps to make the process simpler and more convenient.

When comparing prices on a particular day, check the time of the flights too. Normally expect to pay less when travelling at an unsociable time of day. In addition, some cities are served by more than one airport, so when comparing flights you will need to take into account the extra travelling time and cost to get into the city if a cheaper option is to an airport that is further away.

Once you have found the best online flight deal you will probably want to ask everyone to make their own bookings, but if you do this you will need to make sure they don't forget, as the cheapest seats go quickly. To get the best deals you usually need to book well in advance, often at least four months ahead.

You will probably make the accommodation booking on behalf of the whole group. When you make a hotel reservation some online agents will ask for a deposit or full payment at the time of booking whereas others prefer you to pay the hotel on check-out. You may also be charged if you have to change or cancel your booking; the online agent will usually apply the policy of the hotel you are booked to stay at. This information should be displayed on the website and on the confirmation email you receive once you have booked.

It's worth comparing the quoted room rate on a couple of websites with the hotel's own website, just in case there is a difference and, when booking, try to negotiate a group discount. Before finalising your booking you may wish to check a few reviews of the hotel, which most online agents have posted on their sites. Alternatively, you can visit www.tripadvisor.co.uk. When staying in a city, book accommodation which is conveniently situated, ideally within walking distance of where you will be going out in the evening.

When you make the accommodation booking you will need to decide whether to mention that your group is a stag party. You could just keep quiet and assume that if they don't have a 'no stag parties' message on their website, then they must welcome them. Of course if you do so then you do run the risk of being turned away when you arrive, although this is unlikely to happen in practice.

You may want to arrange some shuttle transport in advance – for example, between the airport and hotel, return trips to any activities and any requirements for the evening out. If you are staying in the UK, rather than use your own cars you might decide that it's easier to hire a minibus, especially if you have a number of journeys to make and a large group is involved.

When travelling abroad, it's a good idea to remind everyone to arrange their own travel insurance and to make sure passports/visas are up to date.

You will find a selection of the online companies offering flights and/or accommodation listed in the appendix (page 150).

DAYTIME ACTIVITIES
To ensure availability aim to book any daytime activities as far in advance as possible, especially if the stag do is to be held

during the summer, which is generally the busiest time of year. For most activities you will only be required to give estimated numbers and a deposit when you make the initial booking. The deposit may be per person and non-refundable, but if someone drops out then most activity providers will allow that person's deposit to be put towards the final payment. As with accommodation, try to negotiate a group discount when you book – a common offer is that the organiser and/or the groom go for free if a certain number of people book. Usually the activity provider will then ask for a final payment up to one month before you visit.

When deciding on the activity, particularly if you are going overseas, you will need to find out how far it is from where you are staying and what transport is available to get you to and from the activity location. You should also check if there are any particular clothing requirements and, if so, let everyone in your group know what they need to bring along.

To ensure you are dealing with a reputable organisation, both in terms of safety (particularly if you are going to be doing something adventurous) and the quality of the service, check whether they belong to any relevant associations, staff qualifications, what insurance cover they have, how long they have been in business, if they have won any awards, and look at testimonials from previous customers.

TICKETS FOR EVENTS
When buying tickets for a daytime or evening event you will probably book directly with the organiser on the venue

website. But don't forget that tickets for many larger events are also sold by online ticketing agents such as Ticketmaster (www.ticketmaster.co.uk), and for some events you can only buy tickets from online agents. If you are not booking directly with the organiser and don't recognise the selling agent, check with the organiser which agents are authorised to sell tickets for the event to ensure that you are buying genuine tickets at their face value. You can also ensure an agent is legitimate by using the website Safeconcerts (www.safeconcerts.com). In addition this site has listings of upcoming events and links to websites of legitimate agents where you can buy tickets.

EVENING PLANS AND OVERALL ITINERARY

Once you have booked the key items listed above you can do some more detailed planning for the evening, which will probably include identifying bars to visit and deciding at what stage you will be eating and where. You can find recommendations of places to go on sites such as TripAdvisor (www.tripadvisor.co.uk) and Beer in the Evening (www. beerintheevening.com). If you are going to book a restaurant it's a good idea to tell them that you are a stag party as they might want to put you somewhere a bit out of the way of the other diners. Of course they may not welcome stag parties at all but it's better to know this in advance so you can book somewhere else rather than wait until you are turned away at the door. If you plan to visit a club later on, check the opening and closing times, whether any particular dress code is required and their policy on stag parties. However welcoming they may sound, as an all-male group it's usually a good idea on the night to split up and arrive at the club in smaller numbers.

Having completed the evening planning, the last task is to put everything together and prepare an overall itinerary for the whole stag do from start to finish. This will then be your reference document to use throughout the event.

ON THE STAG DO

With everything well planned in advance, the stag do itself should run smoothly and all you will have to do on the administration side is to make sure you follow the itinerary and keep everyone together. In this role you are a bit like the teacher on a school trip and as such you may need to be slightly vocal at times – for example, in getting the group moving from one place to the next. As everyone will almost certainly be drinking quite a lot, it's a good idea to set up a kitty at the start of the evening so you don't have to worry about keeping track of whose round it is.

In addition, as the leader of the group you will be expected to sort out any issues that arise. Hopefully there won't be any or any that do arise will just be minor, but as a precaution if you are travelling overseas make sure that you know the relevant emergency services number and have the phone number of the local British Embassy or High Commission to hand.

4.11 STAG PARTY CHECKLIST

The checklist below is intended for a full overseas weekend stag party. If the stag party is in another format such as a day/evening event held locally or you are using a stag party organiser then you will, of course, be able to simplify it accordingly.

Activity	Completed
Agree with your groom the proposed date, list of invitees and what to do (unless it's going to be a surprise)	
Email invitees (or set up a Facebook group) with proposals for the date, what to do and rough cost estimates	
Following feedback, email final plan and confirm stags	
Prepare detailed information on accommodation, flights, activities and associated costs	
Circulate the above to stags and advise them of the booking and payment process	
Book flights (or confirm everyone has made their own booking)	
Book accommodation	
Book main daytime activity	
Book activity for Sunday, if applicable	
Buy tickets for any events	
Book shuttle and any other transport	
Book restaurant	
Prepare overall itinerary	
Ensure you have email confirmations for all bookings	
All required advance payments have been made (e.g. flights, accommodation, activities)	

Activity	Completed
Any payments made by you on behalf of the group have been reimbursed	
Check everyone has travel insurance and passports/visas are up to date	
Buy props	
Decide on icebreaker activities/games	
Remind stags to bring any special clothing required (e.g. for activities or club entry)	
Obtain mobile phone numbers of stags	
Obtain all relevant emergency/British Embassy numbers in local country	
Re-confirm with stags the meeting place for the start of the stag do	
On the stag do itself, follow the itinerary and generally lead the group	

5. THE BEST MAN'S DUTIES ON THE WEDDING DAY

5.1 INTRODUCTION

As well as your specific duties as the best man you will also provide more general support to the bride and groom on the day itself, helping to ensure that everything goes smoothly. This allows them to relax and enjoy the special day without worrying about the organisation. You will therefore be involved in administrative tasks throughout the day – for example, helping to make sure everything runs on time, organising guests, and dealing with any unexpected issues which may arise.

5.2 BEFORE THE CEREMONY

Everything will take longer on the morning of the wedding than you expect, from getting dressed in your formal wear to looking for that important item you need to take with you but cannot find, so make sure you get up early enough to allow for this. If you are not staying with the groom, aim to get to where he is staying early to ensure he is up and about. Remember, you are responsible for getting him to the ceremony on time and you don't want to be rushing around in a last-minute panic. If the buttonholes are not being delivered to where you are staying, you will need to collect these for you and the groom.

Before setting off, double-check that you have the wedding rings, or that the groom has them. If he is leaving straight for the honeymoon at the end of the reception, make sure he also has his luggage, passport and any other travel documents with him.

If the groom has asked you to make some payments on the day, make sure you have the relevant cheques or enough cash. This could include a payment to be made to the vicar or Superintendent Registrar relating to the ceremony costs. You may also have to pay the people who will be providing the entertainment later on, such as any musicians booked to play during the drinks reception or the band playing in the evening. Finally, you should spend a moment checking each of you has your formal wear on properly and make one last check that you have your speech and any props with you.

Your groom will no doubt be feeling some last-minute nerves and it's traditional to stop off for a drink on the way to the wedding for a bit of Dutch courage, ideally at a pub close to where the ceremony is taking place. Make sure it's just the one, though. It's also a good idea to have a packet of mints on you – you don't want to arrive at the ceremony smelling of booze.

The first thing to do once you arrive at the ceremony location is to have a quick word with the ushers to ensure that they understand the seating arrangements and, if it's a church wedding, that they have the Order of Service sheets. Ideally there will be two ushers representing both families available to direct guests to their seats and one usher organising the car parking. The photographer will no doubt already be there and may want a couple of shots of you with the groom. There should be time for the groom to briefly greet the guests before you make your way to the front of the venue ready for the entrance of the bride.

5.3 DURING THE CEREMONY

Your main responsibility during the ceremony will be to look after the rings until you are required to hand them over to the vicar or Superintendent Registrar (you should have received the rings from the groom sometime during the morning prior to the ceremony). Store them in a safe place, such as the inside pocket of your jacket. Resist the temptation to keep taking them out to check if they're still there – the more times you do this, the more likely it is that at some stage they won't be there!

The bride and groom may have decided to have a ring bearer, usually a page boy, in which case he will bring the rings down the aisle, tied onto a cushion. When he arrives, you will just need to untie them and hold onto them until the relevant moment. If it's a church wedding, the vicar will hold an open prayer book in front of you, onto which place the rings. However, it's possible that the bride and groom will go for something more spectacular, such as having the rings delivered during the ceremony by an owl flying in at the relevant moment (I think this is J.K. Rowling's influence!). Apparently there is no need to be trained in falconry – you just have to stick out your hand at the relevant moment. At least in this case you no longer need to worry about losing the rings during the ceremony, just your fingers!

Two witnesses are required to sign the register and it's possible that you may be asked to act as one of them. This takes place either towards or at the end of the ceremony. Photographs are sometimes taken when the register is signed.

5.4 AFTER THE CEREMONY

Once the ceremony is over you will assist in getting the wedding party and guests together for a variety of photographs. The photographer will let you know what individuals are required for each shot, and you should ask the ushers to help you find the relevant people. If the reception is being held at a different location from the ceremony, more photographs will be taken there as well.

One of your roles is to make sure that the wedding follows the itinerary, so if the reception isn't being held at the ceremony venue you should be aware of the approximate time when everyone needs to leave, and at this point you should direct the bride and groom to their waiting car. This is the moment when the guests will usually shower the newlyweds with confetti or rice. There may be a shuttle bus supplied for taking the guests to the reception or they could be making their own way there. You are responsible on the day for making sure that everyone has transport, so either you or one of the ushers should be the last to leave so that no one gets left behind.

5.5 AT THE RECEPTION

To help ensure that the bride and groom are free to focus on socialising and enjoying the reception, make sure any minor queries and issues that arise come to you first to deal with. It may be a good idea to mention this to the venue staff when you arrive.

If there is a seating plan for the meal, organise the ushers so that they are on hand to help guests find their places. You will probably be sitting at the top table (*see also* page 27) and should take responsibility for seating those guests and making sure that everything runs smoothly during the meal.

Master of Ceremonies

Some couples choose to hire a specialist Master of Ceremonies who will make announcements, help organise the guests and keep the wedding running to schedule. However, it's quite common for these duties to be performed by the best man, so if you are acting as the MC, one of your duties is to ensure that the reception keeps to the pre-planned schedule, in particular that the receiving line is formed and that guests pass along it early enough for the meal to begin promptly. Therefore you will need to keep an eye on the time during the drinks reception.

You will have a number of announcements to make at the reception. The bride and groom are the last to enter the room for the reception meal and you will announce their arrival along the lines of 'Ladies and gentlemen, would you please welcome the bride and groom' (although this announcement is sometimes made by a member of staff from the reception venue). After the meal, your next job is to introduce the father of the bride, who will be the first speaker. He could then introduce the groom at the end of his speech and he in turn could introduce you at the end of his own speech. Alternatively, you could introduce the groom and simply stand up and introduce yourself when it's time for you to speak. Either way, you should agree between yourselves beforehand what will happen.

Be sure to check with the bride and groom in advance whether anyone else will be making a speech on the day, because you will need to introduce them as well. Then the final announcement is for the cutting of the cake by the bride and groom. At this point guests often like to take photos, and the official photographer might do so, too.

PRESENTS

The bride and groom may pass to you any presents they receive from guests during the day to look after. They will usually be given these during the drinks reception before the meal. If the presents are not being put on display, you will need to find out from the manager of the reception venue where they can be stored safely.

THE SPEECH

This is the big part of your day and Chapters 6 to 8 (pages 82–148) provide all the guidance you need to help you deliver a great speech. One thing to check before sitting down for the meal is that you have your speech and props with you at the table, and also any emails or cards with messages from people who were unable to make the wedding.

EVENING RECEPTION

After the speeches and the cake there is usually a break before the evening reception starts. If there is any entertainment laid on during this time for the guests, or perhaps just for the children, you will need to ensure that it's all going as planned. The evening party begins with a first dance by the bride and groom and you should make sure that all the guests are aware when this is about to take place. It's a nice gesture if the best man then asks the chief bridesmaid to dance, perhaps towards the end of the first song or for the next one.

By this stage of the wedding, with the pressure of the speech lifted from your shoulders, you should be having a great time and your main role during the evening party is just to keep an eye on things to make sure everything is going smoothly and everyone is enjoying themselves.

THE GOING-AWAY CAR
If there is a going-away car, you and the ushers may wish to decorate it at some point during the evening. In addition, if the bride and groom are going on their honeymoon straight away, make sure their luggage is in the car and that they both have their passports and other documentation with them before they set off.

5.6 AT THE END OF THE EVENING
Once the bride and groom are ready to depart, you should gather the guests to give them a good send-off. After this the guests will probably start to leave. Some guests may be staying at the reception venue. For those who are not, and don't have their own transport, the bride and groom may have arranged for shuttle buses or taxis at the end of the evening, in which

case you should make an announcement informing guests when they will be departing. You will be responsible for making sure that everyone gets back to where they are staying and no one is left stranded at the end of the evening. As the bride and groom may have already left, you should have the phone number of the taxi company being used in case any problems arise. In addition, it's worth having the number of another firm as a backup. Finally, once everyone has gone, take a look around and collect up any items that may have been accidentally left behind by the guests. These you could either leave with the manager of the venue or pass to the mother of the bride to organise the safe return to their owners.

5.7 AFTER THE EVENT

The morning after the wedding there may be a gathering of close family and friends, including the best man, especially if bride and groom haven't yet departed for their honeymoon. Don't forget to hand over any message cards you read out to the bride and groom. After attending this, your help may be required in transporting the wedding presents. Then your last job will be to return any hired clothes.

5.8 WHAT IF THE GROOM WANTS TO CALL THE WEDDING OFF?

No doubt the wedding will go as planned; however, I did mention earlier in this chapter that most grooms will be nervous on their wedding day, and for some this worry may start to make them feel that they would rather not go through with the wedding at all. They may make excuses along the lines of 'Isn't life fine the way it is?', 'Why change things?', 'All that commitment, perhaps I'm too young?', etc., concluding with 'Shouldn't I just call the whole thing off?' Generally your answer to that question if it comes up on the morning of the wedding is a firm 'No'.

It's up to you to steady the groom if this type of panicky thinking starts. At some stage in the planning a lot of men have doubts about getting married – after all, it's a big decision – but as the groom has got to this point, there's probably a 99.999 per cent chance that he's doing the right thing and these last-minute doubts are just caused by the stress of the day. It's your role to listen to him and to keep him calm so that he thinks clearly and focuses on all the positive reasons why he has chosen to get married. Of course, if it becomes apparent that he is part of the 0.001 per cent, then you are in for a crazy day.

5.9 WEDDING DAY CHECKLIST

The following is a reminder of what you need to do on the wedding day and also a few activities relating to the day after.

Activity	Timing
Collect buttonholes, if not delivered to you	Before leaving for the ceremony
Make sure you and the groom have everything with you – speech/props/rings/cheques/cash/honeymoon documents	Before leaving for the ceremony

Activity	Timing
Check that the ushers are directing guests and have the Order of Service sheets	Before the ceremony
Receive the rings from the groom	Before the ceremony
Hand over the rings and sign the register, if required	During the ceremony
Make payments, if required	Throughout the day
Together with the ushers, organise groups for photographs	After the ceremony
Ensure everyone has transport to the reception and that the bride and groom leave on time	After the ceremony
Check everything runs smoothly	Throughout the day
Make sure the receiving line is formed on time and announce the entrance of the bride and groom	At the reception
Announce speakers, make your own speech and announce the cutting of the cake	At the reception
Store the presents	Throughout the reception
With ushers, decorate the going-away car	At the reception
Gather everyone together for the big send-off	End of the evening
Ensure everyone has transport home	End of the evening
Check for any lost items	End of the evening
Attend any morning-after gathering	Day after
Give the bride and groom message cards	Day after
Transport presents, if required	Day after
Return any hired clothes (your own and those of the groom)	Day after

6. PREPARING THE SPEECH – CONTENT

6.1 START NOW!

If you haven't already begun, I recommend that you get together ideas for your speech now. Don't put it off – it will only start to weigh on your mind more and more. I guarantee that once you get something down on paper you will feel a lot better, so my suggestion is that as you work your way through this chapter and the sample speeches, make a few notes and aim to have a summary outline of what you will be including in each part of your speech by the end of it. You could use the structure in the next section as a template and then work on filling in the details over the coming days and weeks. Writing a good speech is a long process and will involve a number of re-writes before you finally have it exactly how you want it.

6.2 TONE, STRUCTURE AND CONTENT

The tone of your speech should be light and amusing, including having a bit of fun at the groom's expense. Your goal is to do this without offending anyone, including the groom and particularly the bride. In terms of overall structure and content, the following is a good template for a best man's speech, but there are no rigid rules so you have the flexibility to do as you wish. I will use this template as I discuss the speech in more detail in this chapter, but you will see in the next chapter that I sometimes vary from this in the sample speeches.

BEGINNING OF THE SPEECH
An icebreaker first joke
Introduce yourself
Compliment the bride and bridesmaids
Thanks on behalf of the bridesmaids, ushers and others

MIDDLE OF THE SPEECH
All about the groom – amusing jokes and anecdotes, gentle teasing

END OF THE SPEECH
Sincere words about being best man and about the groom
Congratulations, best wishes and a few uplifting words for the couple
Toast
Read any messages (these could be read before the toast)

6.3 LENGTH OF THE SPEECH

The best man's speech is usually the longest of the three traditional wedding speeches. This is partly because it should be the most entertaining speech so the audience's attention is easier to hold for longer. As there are no set rules on this, you can decide how long you want to speak. To some extent what you decide probably depends on how much good material you have and how confident you are at public speaking. You don't want to leave the guests feeling short-changed, nor do you want them getting bored and restless. If in doubt, I would go for a shorter speech rather than a longer one – it's better to leave them wanting more rather than drag it out until everyone has lost the will to live! As a guide, I would suggest planning to speak for between five and ten minutes.

6.4 KNOW THE AUDIENCE

THE GUESTS

Before going into more detail about what to include in the speech, it's worth remembering to whom you are giving the speech. Your audience is made up of the family and friends of the bride and groom and therefore they will be a varied group both in terms of age, probably ranging from small children to grandparents, and in terms of what they consider acceptable regarding the content of a speech. Because of this you will have to play it pretty safe in order to avoid causing offence to anyone. In film rating terms, you don't necessarily need to make it a U certificate but you don't want to go too much past 12A.

The dos and don'ts of what to include in the speech are reasonably obvious and I am sure that you, like most people, are sensitive to what is and isn't acceptable. However, it's probably worth going over a few things just as reminders.

Although no one would include explicit sexual jokes in a wedding speech, it's fine to introduce a little light sexual innuendo, and I have used a few examples of this in the sample speeches. However, what people view as acceptable in this area varies a lot, so if you plan to refer to anything with sexual connotations I would test it out first to get a second opinion, although possibly not on someone who attended the stag do!

I would avoid what you might consider to be mild swear words, as some people will probably still find them offensive and won't want to hear them in a speech. Another area to steer well clear of in terms of the speech is ex-girlfriends of the groom, or anecdotes about any of his previous sexual exploits. Of course the same goes for former boyfriends of the bride.

Make sure that your speech is upbeat about marriage. Therefore don't mention subjects like divorce and be careful when choosing wedding quotes and jokes, as many derive their humour from being negative about marriage.

Another area to avoid is linked to this mystery. There has been a murder in the street and the detective is told that the murderer is called John and that he is now playing poker in the pub opposite. The detective goes into the pub and at a table in the corner sits a judge, a doctor, a police officer and the local fire chief all playing poker together. The detective doesn't recognise anyone but immediately goes up and arrests the doctor. How did he know that the doctor committed the crime? The answer is at the end of this section.

As well as being careful not to offend the audience, you will want to make sure that your speech is as inclusive as possible. So use anecdotes that everyone will understand and not in-jokes which only a few people will get, as some of the audience will then feel excluded. Equally, make sure that the audience doesn't need to have a particular piece of knowledge to understand the anecdote (for example, about a particular film or sport) unless you would expect it to be general knowledge, or you can explain the context without going into too much detail and in the process losing the rhythm and focus of the speech.

Back to the mystery: the answer is that all the other poker players were women. Although blatant sexism is generally a thing of the past, some forms of sexual stereotyping do occur, particularly in old wedding jokes, so try to avoid this type of content in your speech. Although it's unlikely to particularly offend anyone, it will make your speech sound a bit dated.

THE BRIDE AND GROOM

In terms of not causing offence, the bride and groom deserve a special mention. The main part of your speech is directed at the groom and making him the centre of a few light-hearted jokes. Gentle teasing and a bit of embarrassment are fine, but don't get carried away and say anything that he might find hurtful or properly embarrassing.

Finally, as it's the bride's day, part of your role is to make sure she enjoys it as much as possible, so double- and then triple-check your speech to ensure there is nothing in it which she would find remotely insulting or embarrassing. When writing your speech, the focus will be on making jokes at the groom's expense, and sometimes you might write something about the groom without realising that it could be interpreted in a different way by the bride, so, to avoid including anything which might inadvertently offend her, consider showing your speech to the chief bridesmaid for review, as she will be more sensitive to how the bride will hear it. Also, without telling the bride the details of your speech, she will be able to reassure her that there is nothing in it for her to worry about. This might be a good idea anyway, as the bride is almost certainly slightly nervous about what you might say, particularly if she doesn't know you that well, or perhaps because she does. Of course, don't tell the groom anything, as you don't want to ruin the element of surprise for him – he needs to be slightly on edge for the whole speech, as that is all part of the fun.

6.5 BEGINNING OF THE SPEECH

Getting up and starting the speech is the hardest part, so you may want to begin with an amusing icebreaker to make an immediate connection with the audience and get a laugh to settle the nerves a bit. Make sure it's short and simple; also easy to understand. For example, here is the opening line from sample speech 1 (page 105):

'For those of you who don't know me, my name is Tom and I am Harry's best man. Take it from me, he's a great bloke, whatever people might say after hearing my speech!'

Alternatively, you could perhaps start with an amusing quote. Here is one that I have used in sample speech 4 (page 115):

'Someone asked me if I was worried about giving the speech. Well, adapting a Woody Allen quote – it's not that I'm afraid of making the speech, it's just that I don't want to be there when it happens!'

You could get the guests' attention by telling them something interesting which happened on the wedding day in history – even better if you turn it into a joke. Here is an example from sample speech 2 (page 108):

'Today is also a historic day, as in 1938 the circus was first televised and transmitted live from Olympia. The audience was informed that they could be seated outside the camera's range if they wanted. Coincidentally, the same offer was made at the show we went to on the stag do!'

Another idea is to mention something topical that has recently been in the news if you can make a joke about it, ideally relating it to marriage. This gives your speech freshness right from the start. As this will be a last-minute addition, make sure you have something in reserve in case nothing comes to mind, though.

If no one introduced you at the start of your speech then you should introduce yourself, either before or after your icebreaker joke. The best man will often compliment the bride at the beginning of his speech, perhaps in part to make sure that he doesn't forget to do so later on. You could do this as part of a light joke at the groom's expense. For instance in sample speech 7 (page 125), I have used the line, 'They do say that opposites attract, and seeing how beautiful Emily is looking today, I'd have to agree!'

At the same time it would be appropriate to say something complimentary about the bridesmaids. In addition, as your speech is a reply on behalf of the bridesmaids to the groom's speech, if he has given the bridesmaids a gift and/or complimented them then you should thank him on their behalf. You could then go on to thank other people such as the ushers and page boy (if there is one) for helping you, and the bride and groom's parents for helping to put on the wedding (although the groom may have already done so).

As you write the speech, remember that you can help strengthen your rapport with the audience if you get them involved as much as possible, for instance by asking a question such as 'Did anyone else not recognise Harry today because he was looking so smart?' The speech will then be more interactive than saying, 'I didn't recognise Harry today because he was looking so smart'.

6.6 MIDDLE OF THE SPEECH

This is the main part of the speech and it's all about the groom. When preparing this, the first thing to do is to make a note of any specific and amusing real-life anecdotes that you already know about the groom's past which may be suitable (if you have a couple of these it will be a lot easier to prepare). Should you be lucky enough to have a lot of stories to choose from, then that's great, but be selective about using them – usually two will suffice. Don't worry if nothing springs to mind at the moment; you may get some inspiration once you start talking to the family and other friends, particularly at family gatherings and on the stag do.

Even if you can't find any specific anecdotes then you can put together a great personal speech by developing material based on things related to the groom, so the next step is to jot down a few of these. For example, they could be general interests (sports, travel, cars, music), achievements (extracts from school reports, certificates obtained, qualifications), current and previous jobs, personality traits or his hobbies (now, or as a child). For these areas you may find material in the sample speeches that you can use directly or adapt. In addition, guidance on writing new material is given in section 6.8 below. Also, props are a great addition to a speech, and in section 6.9 you will find ideas on possible ones to use.

In terms of structure, a popular approach to use for the main part of the speech is to make it a journey through the groom's life, picking up on a few incidents or interests along the way including how you met the groom and maybe how the happy couple met (check if the groom plans to talk about this in his speech first, though). This works well, as everyone listening understands the general structure so hopefully they won't get lost and you are also more likely to remember where to go next in the speech as well. If you decide on this structure there is no need to stick rigidly to it. For example, you could start off by talking about the groom as a child, then move on to discuss his career before discussing his main passion outside work, say a sport, which might lead into talking about how he met the bride (the new passion in his life). There are no set rules for this part of the speech; you just want the outcome to flow smoothly from start to finish so you also need to spend some time thinking about how to link each story together.

Try to ensure that each anecdote you recount isn't too long or it may become a bit rambling, which will leave the audience confused; you might also lose your train of thought, so keep it simple. You will see from the sample speeches in the next chapter that the anecdotes and jokes are generally pretty short. This also helps if one item fails to get a laugh, as you can quickly move on to the next one.

Finally, be on the lookout during the wedding day for anything amusing that is said or done that you could include in the speech as a last-minute anecdote. I have given an example in the introduction to this book from when I was best man and the groom dropped the rings in the church car park. However, don't introduce too much last-minute material into your speech as there is a risk of late changes throwing you off-course during the delivery. One or two incidents will be fine, and certainly don't rely on anything coming up; it's just an added bonus if something does, for it will add to the feeling that the speech is uniquely about that day.

6.7 END OF THE SPEECH

SINCERITY AND THE TOAST

Right, you have almost made it, and after reading Chapter 8 on delivery, on the day itself you will still be talking in a calm, clear, conversational manner, not accelerating up to exit velocity as you race towards the finishing line. Before asking everyone to raise their glasses, the best man usually says a few words as an introduction to build up to the toast. This part of the speech is more about sincerity than being funny. For instance, you may want to thank the groom for making you his best man, to say what an honour it has been for you and to re-affirm that he is a great friend. You could then go on to congratulate the happy couple, wish them all the best for their future together and finish by saying a few uplifting words, possibly using a quote. This will lead nicely into the toast.

Here is an example:

'To end, I would like to thank you, Harry, for being such a great friend over the years and for asking me to be your best man – it's been an honour. I'd also like to congratulate you and Emily on your marriage and to wish you all the very best for a fantastic future together. Someone once said, 'In the opinion of the world marriage ends all, as it does in comedy. The truth is precisely the opposite: it begins all'. And I know how much we have all enjoyed being here for the beginning. So now, ladies and gentlemen, would you please be upstanding and raise your glasses. I'd like to propose a toast – to the bride and groom!' [To which everyone replies, 'The bride and groom!']

In fact it isn't strictly necessary for the best man to propose a toast at all, but it has become the norm and it's a nice way to round off the speech. Although the father of the bride will have already made a toast to the bride and groom it is usual nowadays for the best man to end his speech by making a toast to them as well. Alternatively, you could propose a toast to absent friends or to the parents of the bride and groom, particularly if they have been heavily involved in organising and paying for the wedding. Perhaps the reception is being held in a marquee in the bride's parents' garden, in which case you could thank them and then propose a toast to the parents of the bride. It's up to you to decide what you feel is most appropriate for the circumstances. If you are unsure, you could stick with a toast to the bride and groom or ask if there is a particular toast that they would like you to give as an alternative.

There are many more examples of how to finish off the speech in the sample speeches in the next chapter, including toasts not proposed to the bride and groom. You will also see from these that it's fine to make the ending of the speech more informal if you prefer and to add a touch of humour.

MESSAGES

Some invitees will not have been able to make the wedding and may have sent their best wishes by email or in cards, and as best man you will be expected to read these messages out. The messages can be a bit difficult to fit into your speech without losing the flow so one option is to leave them until after you have made your toast at the end of the speech. To make this part a little more lively and interesting you could add a made-up message. An example from sample speech 8 (page 129) is, 'Here's one from David Cameron and Nick Clegg, wishing you all the best, and their advice for a great partnership is never to discuss politics in the bedroom … and both their marriages have lasted a long time, so sound advice!'

6.8 WRITING NEW MATERIAL

For the speech, in addition to recounting amusing incidents from the groom's past and using or adapting some of the material in this book, you could write something completely new, based on a subject connected to the groom. As an example I will go through something I came up with that will give you a feel for the process I use, which may be helpful.

A friend recently mentioned that she was to be chief bridesmaid at a wedding and we talked about the best man's speech and what he might say. She mentioned in passing that the groom and the best man did archery together. As I hadn't written any material about archery before, I thought I would have a go at writing something. The first thing I do with any new subject is to write down related words or phrases that come into my head, so for archery I came up with the following:

Bow and Arrows, Cupid, Target, Robin Hood.

I then try to think of things connected with the words and how I might develop them to form the basis of a joke or anecdote.

Bow and Arrows: The word 'arrows' made me think of the Royal Air Force Red Arrows team. I thought that The Red Arrows could be the name of an archery team, so maybe some sort of confusion between the two might be turned into a joke.

Cupid: This made me think of matchmaking, so perhaps Cupid could be built into how the bride and groom got together. Maybe I could use a picture of Cupid with his bow and arrow in some sort of groom-as-a-baby story.

Target: I thought of archers shooting at targets, and then the image of someone standing with an apple on his head came into my mind. This made me think it would be funny if the best man suggested this as part of the wedding entertainment.

Robin Hood: Made me think of men wearing tights and also made me want to see the film again – the classic swashbuckling 1938 version with Errol Flynn of course, not the remakes.

I then spent some time developing these ideas into a speech extract. Much of this time is spent in trying to write in a way so that the audience won't be able to second guess where you are going next. You are playing a game of cat and mouse with them and you are the mouse. This is because generally for jokes to work, you need that element of surprise. You don't want the audience to work out your punch line before you say it; the more unexpected it is, the funnier it will be (which is probably why jokes are rarely funny the second time you hear them). I did add the cat and mouse analogy for a reason, as I wanted to make another point, which is that part of what you are doing when writing the speech is trying to tell the story in such a way as to create a mental image in the audience's mind of what is going on, thereby making it more interesting and bringing the story to life.

I then had to decide on the order in which to use the ideas and how to link them together. It helps the flow of a speech if you can link one item to the next. For instance, I was wondering how to get from talking about Robin Hood to discussing the bride and groom and how they got together and you will see how I came up with the idea of using Maid Marian as the link. This ended up being quite useful too, as it allowed me to compliment the bride at the same time. Likewise you will see that I mention the 'flypast' again at the start of the final section to get a link from the Red Arrows part to the apples-on-heads bit. These links not only help to make the speech flow more smoothly, they also act as reminders of where to go next when you are actually delivering it.

As I was writing the speech I was also saying it aloud to ensure my words combined well and sounded natural when spoken. I discuss delivering the speech in Chapter 8, but the groundwork to allow you to get the delivery right is to have a well-prepared speech. After a few re-writes I finally had down what I wanted to say.

So here is what I came up with:

'As you know, Harry was into archery from an early age [show painting of naked Cupid with Harry's face]*; here he is as a baby, showing off his bow and arrows. It's certainly a relief to all of us that he now keeps his clothes on when competing. This interest continued as he got older. I guess, like me, you too were drawn to men wearing tights growing up – I'm talking mainly to the guys now, of course. But while most of us wanted to be Spiderman or Superman, Harry's hero was Robin Hood and like Robin Hood with Maid Marian, Harry has also found himself a beautiful woman, Emily, to join him on his adventures. And how did this romance begin? Did Harry shoot his very own Cupid's arrow at Emily's heart in the hope of making her fall for him? Well, if he did, with his accuracy he must have been standing pretty close to her to get a hit! But whatever he did, it worked, as Emily agreed to marry him – even after the disappointment of finding out that she wouldn't*

get an RAF flypast on her wedding day. That was following clarification from Harry about which Red Arrows team he did actually know.

'So to compensate for no flypast today, for the pre-evening entertainment you'll be pleased to hear that I've brought along my bow and arrows, and some apples. For the benefit of any children who don't know the story of William Tell, *it's all pretty straightforward. You put the apple on your head, your parents sign a disclaimer, and I then shoot the arrow at the apple. If I miss, you get to keep the apple. I can see some of you are beginning to look worried, but there's no need – there are plenty of apples to go round. Although a word of advice: try to get one of my early slots before the alcohol starts to kick in.'*

Just to highlight the point I made above about needing the element of surprise, in the penultimate sentence which started, *'I can see some of you are beginning to look worried, but there's no need'*, the audience might expect me to then say something reassuring about my skills or that I was only joking, but by finishing with *'there are plenty of apples to go round'*, this would hopefully have taken people by surprise and got a laugh.

One point about the extract above is that although it sounds quite personal, there is nothing too specific about the groom in it, apart from his interest in archery. So when writing your own speech, don't worry if you haven't found any good anecdotes from the groom's past; you can still give a personal speech without them; just work with what you do know about him.

In a best man's speech there is nothing to stop you inventing the odd thing for comic effect. For example, the Red Arrows flypast bit is made up, but that's fine as it's obvious that it wouldn't be true but is simply a joke. However, if you are telling real-life anecdotes then you don't want to stretch the truth too far. A little exaggeration is fine, but the basic facts should be correct – unless of course you indicate that what you are saying may not be true. For example, in the extract above I have said that the groom liked Robin Hood, but if I didn't know this then I could have said 'Rumour has it that Harry's hero was Robin Hood', which casts an element of doubt.

Something else that I referred to earlier (page 89) and have used here is to involve the audience. This will make them feel part of the story and helps break down barriers, so I have said *'I guess like me, you too were drawn to men wearing tights growing up – I'm talking mainly to the guys now, of course'* instead of something along the lines of *'All boys were drawn to men wearing tights growing up'.*

One final point, which is also a lead-in to the next section, relates to the use of props. In the above extract there is one prop used – the image of Cupid. I think props are great to add comic impact, so although I probably wouldn't recommend bringing in a bow and arrow, the best man could take along a few apples and then say 'You'll be pleased to hear that I have my bow and arrows outside and I also have a few of these' before showing the apples. Having a prop almost always makes a joke funnier.

6.9 PROPS

People like props. When I was best man I remember going to the top table and passing a guest who saw my bag of stuff and excitedly said, 'Ooh, props!' This is because props add excitement to a speech, a sense of theatre and drama. As they can be great fun you will get a big laugh from them, so I would definitely recommend using at least one. The other great thing about props is that they are visual, so if you are worried that you are not very good at telling jokes it doesn't matter, as here is a way of getting a laugh without having to tell a joke – for instance, if the prop is a funny hat and it is now sitting on the groom's head. I have given a few prop ideas below, and, having already mentioned hats, I will start with them.

HATS

The hat choice is large; you just need to find a relevant subject and an appropriate hat to go with it. For example, in sample speech 9 (page 132), the groom is presented with a cork hat, as the couple are going to Australia on their honeymoon, and in sample speech 5 (page 119), it's a chef's hat, as the story relates to the groom's cooking abilities. As it's a wedding, you can decorate the hat in the same way as you would the going-away car. So write 'Just Married' on it, spray with shaving cream and attach a few cans on the back.

Hats are not the only option; you could also get the groom a special going-away jacket with much the same decoration on the back. In addition, there is nothing to stop you wearing a hat yourself or some other item of clothing if it will enhance the story you are telling.

SPORTS SHIRT

This involves presenting the bride with a sports shirt of the team that the groom supports. For example, if the groom is a big Arsenal fan you could present the bride with one of their football shirts, and, where the player's name normally goes on the back of the shirt, add her new married name, e.g. 'Mrs Wright' (see sample speech 3, page 112). Of course, don't forget to check before the wedding that the bride is taking the groom's surname and not keeping her maiden name.

THE SURPRISE

This involves having something hidden in a bag that you are going to give the newlyweds – for example, for the honeymoon – and building suspense while you talk about it. You can add to the tension if the audience feels that what you are about to produce from the bag is inappropriate, and then, when it isn't, you will get a laugh, from surprise and relief (see sample speeches 4 and 7, pages 115 and 125).

PICTURES OF THE GROOM

A popular prop is to show an embarrassing picture of the groom, possibly from his childhood, or maybe a picture that you are pretending is of the groom (e.g. the picture of Cupid as previously mentioned on page 96).

SLIDE SHOW OR VIDEO

If the reception venue has the appropriate equipment you might consider including in your speech a slide show or a video showing the groom at different times in his life. You could either show this as you go through your speech at relevant points or save it for the end. An alternative is to make an entertaining video with some of the couple's friends – for instance, telling anecdotes related to the bride and groom, re-enacting scenes from their relationship or miming to an appropriate song. With this idea you have the possibility to do something very creative and original. Make sure, however, that whatever you include won't detract from the speech but will enhance it. It needs to be incorporated in a way that still allows the speech to flow smoothly from start to finish, so it may be better to show it at the end before the toast. If you plan to go down this route it's a good idea to visit the venue before the wedding and have a practice run so you know everything will work on the day.

SOMETHING FROM HIS CHILDHOOD

Did the groom have any embarrassing toys as a child? If you didn't know him back then, ask the family, and if there was something, maybe they still have it somewhere in the loft. Alternatively, maybe he made something as a child, say in art or woodwork, which the family still has and which you could use to show off his talents. Perhaps the family has kept some of his old school reports, which can often be a good source of material.

MISCELLANEOUS

There are many potential props out there that could be used, so once you have written your speech it's worth spending some time thinking if any of the stories could be enhanced by the introduction of a prop. You may find inspiration from the sample speeches in the next chapter, where I have used a variety of miscellaneous props. Also, keep a lookout for day-to-day objects connected with the groom and his interests, which might be amusing to use. Maybe when you are round at his place you may get a flash of inspiration, particularly as a lot of men tend to hoard their old stuff.

6.10 QUOTES

At the end of your speech before the toast you might consider using a quote with an uplifting or insightful message about marriage or relationships. Here are a few examples that I have used in the sample speeches. If you are looking for other possible quotes to include in your speech, you will find a large selection online – for example, try www.brainyquote.com or www.quotegarden.com.

If you have love, you don't need to have anything else, and if you don't have it, it doesn't matter much what else you have (Sir James M. Barrie) (speech 5).

Friendship is the source of the greatest pleasures, and without friends even the most agreeable pursuits become tedious (Saint Thomas Aquinas) (speech 4).

Are we not like two volumes of one book? (Marceline Desbordes-Valmore) (speech 9).

My most brilliant achievement was my ability to be able to persuade my wife to marry me (Sir Winston Churchill) (speech 3).

In the opinion of the world marriage ends all, as it does in comedy. The truth is precisely the opposite: it begins all (Anne Sophie Swetchine)

To keep your marriage brimming, with love in the loving cup, whenever you're wrong admit it; whenever you're right, shut up (Ogden Nash) (speech 10)

You don't need to limit yourself to quotes relating to marriage and relationships; other quotes that you come across could potentially be used if they relate to what you are discussing in the speech, or, if you really like a particular quote, you could try and write the speech in a way that allows you to use it without it seeming out of place. Casting your net wider will certainly help if you are looking for more humorous quotes, as most marriage and relationship ones get their humour from being jokingly negative so they are not particularly suitable, and most people will almost certainly have heard the funnier ones before anyway. You will see in the sample speeches in the next chapter that I have used general quotes from a variety of sources including Woody Allen, Billy Connolly and Homer Simpson.

6.11 ONLINE MATERIAL

If you want to see examples of actual speeches given by other best men you will find some of these posted online (for example, www.hitched.co.uk). In addition, you will also find wedding videos of best man speeches on YouTube. If you are thinking of using any material you find, bear in mind that, just because someone else has used it, this doesn't automatically mean it's appropriate for your wedding audience, so use your own judgement when deciding whether or not to use any material.

6.12 ANNIVERSARIES

Most wedding anniversaries have traditional names associated with them and you may wish to refer to them in your speech (see sample speech 8 on page 129 for an example), so here are the names of the early anniversaries and other significant ones.

1st	Paper
2nd	Cotton
3rd	Leather
4th	Fruit and flowers
5th	Wood
10th	Tin
25th	Silver
40th	Ruby
50th	Gold
60th	Diamond
70th	Platinum

7. SAMPLE SPEECHES

For this chapter I have written ten sample speeches, all with completely original material that will bring to life many of the ideas I have discussed in the previous chapter. Seeing full-length speeches will hopefully give you a feel for how to structure your own speech and also provide you with ideas for the type of material you could include.

WEDDING SPEECH No. 1

Good afternoon, ladies and gentlemen. For those of you who don't know me, my name is Tom and I am Harry's best man. Take it from me, he's a great bloke, whatever people might say after hearing my speech.

Well, it's quite an impressive turnout today, certainly better than the handful of people I ended up speaking to last time I was best man, although the numbers were similar at the start of the speech. I think perhaps in hindsight demonstrating one of the groom's hobbies with a live sheep was a mistake, even though I'd practised that bit the most! Thing was, the sheep wouldn't keep still, so shearing it was never going to be easy. So don't worry, all the props today are dead.

So how would I describe Harry? Well, on the plus side he is very reliable and dependable, but he does like everything to be in order and he's not too keen on change. For instance, if

I told him that the world would end in a few minutes, what would he do? First, he would probably remind me that he doesn't like surprises, but of course he would want to spend the time with Emily; I also know he'd prefer to be at home, as the few minutes remaining would be plenty of time for his last activity, which would be to take the final utility readings and make sure the water was turned off at the mains. Although he is slowly getting more adventurous – for instance, yesterday after we collected our formal wear we tried the new barbers that has just opened in town, called 'Hair Today' and, looking at Harry's cut, probably gone tomorrow.

So what else can I tell you about Harry? Well, you can tell a lot about someone from talking to family and friends, but to get the complete picture you really need to take a look at their medical records. So I talked with Harry's doctor, who kindly passed them on to me and I have them here. Obviously she was slightly concerned about confidentiality, so Harry, if you wouldn't mind putting these on for a minute [pass him some headphones].

Seems Harry is quite a frequent visitor to Dr Jones, a bit of a hypochondriac. In fact, by last September, the notes say that Dr Jones was considering taking on extra staff to cope with the workload. Indeed, with the honeymoon coming up, the surgery is looking forward to the break, even though they were quite surprised to be invited.

Anyway, having looked through the notes, I'm afraid it's not good news. Looks like the frostbite in his toes from the skiing trip is worse than they thought and they're not sure if they can save the foot [give groom a smile and thumbs-up sign]. Just thought you should know in case any of you had been planning on getting him slippers for Christmas.

[Get groom to take headphones off.] Just saying to Emily, how lucky she is to have such a healthy husband. You've given up football, haven't you?

In fact, Harry is actually very fit and enjoys most sport. He's a particularly good runner and also very reliable. So, Emily, if you ever consider trading him in as one lady owner, you should get a pretty good price.

You may not be aware, but I am giving my services for free today. I will, however, have a stall set up outside afterwards selling souvenirs. While I have your attention I'd just like to show you one of the items for which I'll be taking orders: the commemorative plate [get out plate with the Duke and Duchess of Cambridge on it]. The more observant among you will notice a difference in the happy couple. This is of course the Kate and William – the actual ones of Emily and Harry will be available in the next few weeks. There will also be a separate one of the best man, which I expect to be very popular. In fact I have an advance copy here [show plate with your photo in formal wear on it, together with details of the wedding]. I know, Harry, you were wondering what I'd got you and Emily as a wedding present [present plate to bride and groom].

I know some of Harry's friends here today haven't seen him for a long time, so I won't keep you much more as I'm sure you've been looking forward to catching up and finding out what he's done over the last few years … with the money you lent him.

Before I finish, I would like to say how beautiful you are looking, Emily, and how pleased I am that you are marrying Harry ... as I know you could have done a lot better. I'd also like to thank you, Harry, on behalf of the bridesmaids for your kind words. I would also agree that the bridesmaids are looking lovely and I know I'm not alone in being impressed by the dresses, especially as the colour is the same as the Arsenal away kit.

There are a couple of cards from people who can't be here today which I would like to read out [read out messages]. Here is one from Ant & Dec wishing you all the best and giving you this piece of advice, which has worked for them: 'never get on the wrong side of your partner'.

Jane Austen wrote that a single man in possession of a good fortune must be in want of a wife, and those of us who know Harry would agree how much truer this is for the man who has virtually nothing. And he certainly looks pretty happy today! So I'd like to end by thanking you, Harry, for making me your best man, it's been a real honour; and to wish you and Emily all the very best for your future together. So, ladies and gentlemen, I'd now like to ask you to please be upstanding and raise your glasses as I'd like to propose a toast: to Emily and Harry, the bride and groom.

WEDDING SPEECH No. 2

Good afternoon, ladies and gentlemen. Today is also a historic day as in 1938 the circus was first televised and transmitted live from Olympia. The audience was informed that they could be seated out of the camera's range if they wanted. Coincidentally, the same offer was made at the show we attended on the stag do.

On behalf of the bridesmaids I'd like to thank you, Harry, for the compliments and for their gifts. I guess my present must be parked outside?

For those people I haven't met yet my name is Tom and I'm the best man. Must say until yesterday I was cruising in my role, wondering what all the fuss was about. Then when I arrived at Harry's house he gave me a rather long 'to do' list, which somewhat worryingly included: run the florist over, take a few shots if any guests drop by, deal with any last requests from the family and then confirm arrangements with the priest. Apart from sounding as if we were about to make a Tarantino movie, I realised what a lot I had to do, so I was really lucky to have some great accomplices. So I'd like to take this opportunity to thank the ushers for all their support. I know many of you were impressed with the speed at which they got you parked when you arrived at the church, particularly when compared to how long it took you to get out of the car park afterwards. And later on I will be raising a toast to absent friends, many of whom I believe are still at the church. No, only joking – most have now made it to the ring road.

So what can I tell you about Harry? Well, we grew up together and I learnt a lot from him over the years, just by observing his mistakes. But to his credit by following the rule that 'if at first you don't succeed, give up', he has never made the same mistake twice, and that, by the way, is just one of the many life guidance tips he has picked up from Homer Simpson. And by following this rule he has also ended up with what one recruitment consultant describes as 'an impressively varied and comprehensive CV'. But he finally found his calling in life, which was to become a teacher. As they say, you never forget a good teacher and I think from all the cards he's received today from former students it proves that you tend to remember the other ones as well! Still, it was encouraging to hear that one or two of them are finally in work.

As you probably know, when not working Harry likes to play golf. He did get a 'hole-in-one' once – luckily for him, when he finished the only person around to buy drinks for was the man in the kiosk when he handed the putter back. But as anyone who has seen him playing at our club will know, that's not actually why we call him 'crazy golf'. Certainly for your sake, Emily, I hope his driving in the car is better than on the golf course. Although if you see Harry on the roads, it's more likely that he will be racing on his bike and his cycling times are improving. He says this is from studying other cyclists – I guess because he spends so much time in competitions behind them. Anyway Harry, I know Emily's worried that you won't be able to keep up with her when you're out cycling on the honeymoon, so to inspire you, I have bought you your own yellow jersey [show yellow jersey with 'addicted to speed' on the back] – this is one of Lance Armstrong's old ones.

So why has Emily married Harry, if not for his sporting prowess? Was it because of the way he throws his money around? Well, I have heard it said that there's generous, very generous and then there's Harry, although I've never heard it said in that order. If you do go out for a beer with him, on the plus side he'll always open the pub door for you so you can get to the bar first. Although he may not buy the first round, he always keeps track and knows when it's his turn to get the round. And he will get it, if the rest of us can be bothered to try and find him. But actually, Harry isn't stingy at all. In fact, I've seen him pay for a taxi just to go a couple of hundred yards. Some people also say he is lazy, but I've seen no evidence.

Anyway Emily, whatever the reason for marrying him, I think I speak for all of his friends when I say thanks for taking him off our hands, especially as we all know that the older ones are always harder to place – as Harry himself found out while he was registered on Carbon Dating, the Internet relationship website for old fossils. But I would say that Emily and Harry look the perfect couple today. Emily is looking even more beautiful than usual and Harry isn't looking too bad either. I take some credit for that, having helped him to get dressed in his formal wear this morning. All those episodes of *Downton Abbey* I've been made to sit through by Chloe seem to have paid off.

Like everyone else I've had a brilliant day today, and Harry, I'm very pleased that you asked me to be your best man and to be part of this day; it's been an honour. You're a great friend, and I hope after this speech, one who will still be talking to me. I'd now like to finish by proposing a toast to absent friends. It's good to see that so many of you made it today, particularly considering I was giving the best man's speech – an excellent reflection of just how popular Emily and Harry are. But there are a few friends of theirs who haven't been able to make it today. Therefore would you please be upstanding and raise a glass as I would now like to propose a toast: to absent friends.

WEDDING SPEECH No. 3

Good afternoon, ladies and gentlemen. This is definitely a special day because as well as Emily and Harry getting married, on 3 April 1367, King Henry IV was born. At the same time, his father was victorious in Spain with the Black Prince and missed the birth. I bet he regretted bothering to attend all those antenatal classes!

I'd like to start by thanking Harry on behalf of the bridesmaids for their gifts and I would also agree that they look fantastic. I'd like to say as well what a lucky guy you are to be marrying Emily, who looks stunning today. I've known Harry for a long time, twenty years in fact. Actually it's twenty years this month, so happy anniversary, Harry! But please don't raise your glasses yet as we are here to celebrate something else as well today. So, I knew Harry growing up and back then we had only one thing on our minds, pretty much the same as now, and that was … football. Although we are about the same age, Harry was in the year below me at school, which he explained was because he'd taken a gap year. So I didn't actually see too much of him during school time – a similar comment was made by the teaching staff as well.

But we were always together after school, kicking a ball around. Harry was pretty good at 'Keepy-Uppy'. Back then he could keep going for ten minutes or so. I guess, Harry, you'd struggle to Keepy-Uppy for more than a couple of minutes now, if at all. Anyway, luckily for you, Emily isn't marrying you for your Keepy-Uppy ability or she'll be very disappointed.

Talking of football, as a number of you know, Harry is a keen Arsenal fan, and Emily, as well as being welcomed into the Wright family today, I'd also like to welcome you into the slightly larger family of Arsenal fans and to make this small presentation to you.

[Get out replica shirt and present to the bride; if she is taking the groom's surname, have her new married name, e.g. 'Mrs Wright', printed where the player's name normally goes on the back of the shirt.]

There's no need to try it on now, although I know that Harry was keen that you had it in time for tonight. In fact there are some rules about wearing it.

1. It needs to be worn for all match days, whether or not you are attending the game.

2. Specially nominated days including [popular player]'s birthday and Harry's birthday – daytime optional.

3. The duration of any package holiday you take to a Mediterranean resort.

So what else can I tell you about Harry? Well, in terms of flaws in his character or embarrassing moments in his life, there is surprisingly little to tell … according to the letter I've received from his lawyers. But actually he is a good bloke. I mean, I've never seen him helping old ladies across the road or anything like that, but then again I've never seen him mug one either. Anyway, he doesn't have a criminal record and he's never been arrested (in fact I don't think they've ever been close to catching him). So based on the lawyers' advice I thought it might be a good idea to talk about Harry's attributes and after only a few days I managed to come up with three. I'm sure if we all put our minds together, by the end of the evening we'd be able to come up with one or two more. Anyway, don't worry if all that sounds like too much hard work because I'm not going to ask you to do it. So here are my three:

1. Generosity: Harry has been generous over the years, giving presents to family and friends, and so it's nice today to see the roles reversed and him getting so many presents back. It's good to see most of them are still in their original packaging as well. Harry's also a big giver to charity … indirectly through the lottery. But I don't believe he's playing it just to win – if he was, he'd pick whole numbers like the rest of us! Harry's even got himself a donor card – I think he was tempted by the fact that there is no annual charge. He's also given blood and, more recently, a DNA sample – so an all-round generous bloke.

2. Trustworthiness: Billy Connolly said, 'Never trust a man who, when left alone with a tea cosy, doesn't try it on.' And if that's the test of trustworthiness, Harry would pass within seconds.

3. Cleanliness: I mention this not because Harry necessarily has better general hygiene standards than you or me, but just

because of how far he's come. It was only recently that you'd take a risk going round to his place if your inoculations weren't up to date. Not any more, though and I think we have Emily to thank for that.

As well as these attributes you may also be surprised to hear that Harry has something in common with the great Sir Winston Churchill, who by the way will soon be the new face on the £5 note, appearing with one of his well-known quotes, which is, 'I have nothing to offer but blood, toil, tears and sweat'. However, it's not actually the wedding vows I'm referring to, but achievements, as Churchill also once said, 'My most brilliant achievement was my ability to be able to persuade my wife to marry me', and that of course is Harry's as well, and to quote Churchill again, this is definitely Harry's 'finest hour'.

So I think the omens are good for Emily and Harry, particularly as I don't think they've argued all the time they've been married, and there aren't many married couples who can honestly say that. I know they will have a fantastic future together. So can I ask you now to please be upstanding and raise your glasses as I would like to propose a toast: to the bride and groom.

WEDDING SPEECH No. 4

Good afternoon, ladies and gentlemen. Someone asked me earlier if I was worried about the speech. Well, adapting a Woody Allen quote, 'It's not that I'm afraid of making the speech. It's just that I don't want to be there when it happens'

– I definitely felt the urge to run away a few minutes ago. But then I remembered what a great friend Harry is, and if I didn't give the speech then I'd really be letting him … off the hook!

So what can I tell you about Harry? Well, we did grow up together and one of his big interests growing up was trains, particularly the local train service. In fact he could tell you the full details of all the timetables, including stopping points and whether a buffet service was available. And he still takes an interest – I know how excited he was a few weeks ago when he overheard Emily talking about maybe having a wedding train. So I thought it would be a nice idea today if you have arrived here by train, if you wouldn't mind leaving your outward bound ticket – it will be a cracking souvenir of the day for Harry. I'll leave a collecting box in the main hall, by the anorak stand.

After growing up in Swindon, Harry chose to go to Birmingham University and after great deliberations decided on an appropriate course: he'd take the First Great Western service to Oxford via Didcot Parkway and then change for the Cross Country service to Birmingham.

It was while at university that Harry met Emily – in fact it was at one of Charlotte's many dinner parties. Charlotte told Emily she had this fantastic guy she wanted her to meet – talk about building up expectations. Anyway, when he had to drop out she invited Harry along instead. But the evening couldn't have gone better: Harry was really impressed with Emily, and Emily was really impressed with Charlotte's coq au vin, so when he called her up a few days later she surprisingly agreed to go out on a date with him, even after he'd reminded her who he was. And here we are today, seven years later, celebrating that same relationship, appropriately over another plate of chicken.

Emily and Harry are flying off on their honeymoon later on, and I think we all know what in-flight meal they'll choose. Emily initially agreed that the honeymoon should be a surprise, but she soon changed her mind. I suspect that she probably discovered a cheap and cheerful campsite brochure hidden down the back of the sofa because Harry does like to get a bargain, as those of us who have ever received a present from him will testify. Talking of presents from Harry, when Emily started getting them she surprised us all by putting them on the mantelpiece, as the family normally put them … on eBay! And apparently they're still there – well, at least they were the last time Emily looked … when she was moving out of the flat last year. Anyway I mentioned camping as a honeymoon possibility as I know Harry enjoys it, although I have to say that I'm not so keen. In fact I think one of the key things that distinguishes us from the rest of the animal kingdom is that we live indoors. And in particular for someone like Harry, you sleep outside and the boundaries become very blurry indeed. I can see that those of you who saw Harry eating his meal earlier are nodding.

Talking about the honeymoon [get out small plastic bag]. Just in case in the excitement and rush to get ready for the wedding you have forgotten to pack some honeymoon essentials, I've popped down to the chemist to pick something up for you. I've actually bought a packet of six but now I'm wondering if that's going to be enough as I expect you'll use a couple every night in bed. And I've read the packet and they don't recommend you re-use them. These actually have extra padding for more comfort [get out earplugs]. Anyway they're guaranteed to cut out almost all noise, so hopefully, Emily, you won't be too bothered by Harry's snoring. Just so you don't feel left out, Harry, I've got you something for the honeymoon as well. It's a magazine [show plastic bag with magazine in it, but hidden]. You may not know it, but Harry's not a big reader. In his view, if a book is that good they'll make a film of it, and he's happy to wait (in fact, the only reading test I think he's passed was at the opticians). But not to worry, Harry – this one is mainly pictures, but to avoid embarrassment I suggest you read this magazine when you're on your own [then pull a trains magazine out of the bag and give to the groom].

Before I finish, I have an announcement from the hotel that unfortunately due to health and safety regulations Emily won't be allowed to throw her bouquet in case anyone gets injured. But not to worry as I've organised a raffle for it instead and also added a couple of extra prizes to the draw. So if you miss out on the bouquet, you might still win the second prize: the much sought-after first dance of the evening with Jack, the chief usher. And the winner of the third prize will have a choice: spend a Saturday night on a date with Josh, the other usher, or do ten hours' community service.

I would like to say, Harry, what a great honour it has been to be your best man. St Thomas Aquinas said, 'Friendship is the source of the greatest pleasures, and without friends even the most agreeable pursuits become tedious', and I've certainly really appreciated your friendship over the years. And I couldn't be more pleased that you have found such a fantastic person as Emily to share your life with, who I might add is looking beautiful today.

We all look forward to a wedding – for me it's the opportunity to prove once again that I can't dance. Anyway I think you'll agree that this one has definitely lived up to expectations and it has been a great day, and a lot of that is thanks to Emily's parents, Jane and Rob. So, I will now ask you to join me and raise a glass as I would like to propose a toast: to Emily's parents, Jane and Rob.

WEDDING SPEECH No. 5

Good afternoon, ladies and gentlemen. My name is Tom and I'm Harry's best man, but possibly only until the end of this speech so I've put the chief usher on standby.

One of the nicest things today is to see the two families and two sets of friends getting on so well together so I'm not sure why someone insisted there was segregation in the church earlier. Mind you, having seen the state of some of the guys on the stag do, I wouldn't have been at all surprised if the police had asked us to bring forward the 3 o'clock kick-off for the service to just before the pubs opened.

On the subject of Harry's male friends they are not actually as dodgy as they look – in fact they're a pretty honest and trustworthy bunch. Just thought I should clarify that as I know some of you have been wondering if they were the reason why the wedding presents haven't been put on display. So having put your minds at rest, if any of you want to get your jewellery back out of the hotel safe to wear this evening, there will be a short break after my speech.

As a lot of you know, Harry is a keen photographer. He was all set to take the photos today, until Emily made it clear that she was not happy to have a stand-in, even for the distance shots. He also likes taking videos … of his holidays. If you get invited round to watch his holiday videos you'll certainly be impressed by how many film-making techniques he is familiar with, it's just a pity that editing isn't one of them, so make sure you allow a whole evening. My advice is to arrive a good thirty minutes late – that way you will at least miss the trailers for the next trip. You may be surprised that there isn't a video being made of today, but as Harry explained to me earlier, why pay for a videographer when the hotel has extensive CCTV coverage and they told him that his deal is fully inclusive?

I'd now like to talk about what makes a good marriage. Well, I think it's good to have things in common. So what have Emily and Harry got in common? Well, they both like DIY. Emily bought her place a couple of years ago and did it up. Harry bought his home many years ago and is still doing it up – in fact, the repainting of the lounge is still not complete. Even Michelangelo was able to finish off the Sistine Chapel in quicker time, although I guess he was only doing the ceiling!

Emily and Harry are now combining their DIY skills and moving into a new house together which needs complete refurbishment and it's a pretty big place. For those of you who haven't seen it yet, to give you an idea of the size … St Paul's Cathedral … well, that's bigger than Emily and Harry's … but their place has more bedrooms. Emily, now that you're moving in with Harry and bringing all your stuff, you might want to take the precaution of getting a small safe. Not that Harry will nick any of your stuff, although he might want to try a few things on, but he isn't particularly security conscious so you'll end up spending your life locking up after him.

I think in a relationship, as well as having things in common, it's good to be able to enjoy your own space. In Emily and Harry's case this will be possible even in the house, for you'll rarely see Harry in the bathroom or the kitchen. Although Harry says he'll share the bathroom chores, by that he means he'll put the toilet seat up and Emily can put it down again. On that subject I have a solution that will in fact stop all couples arguing about the toilet seat position: include individual urinals as part of bathroom suites. Also, I think all of us blokes will love it, as every night it will feel like we're in the pub. In addition, 'his and hers' toilets will give couples something else to do together. So I know you were wondering what I'd bought you as a wedding present – well, that's not it! Thought I'd just let you know so you're not too disappointed when you get back to the house from the honeymoon.

Some of us would say it's probably a good thing that Harry does stay out of the kitchen, as there is something slightly worrying about hearing the words 'Harry' and 'cooking' in the same sentence. Actually I think he does occasionally cook, as he's often bragging about how good his pork tender loins are. Emily has told me that Harry will be expected to do his fair share of the cooking once she's installed smoke alarms. Anyway Harry, to ensure you at least look the part, I've got you a small gift. [Present groom with a chef's hat with 'Just Married' written on it, empty tins of beans attached to the back and sprayed with shaving cream.] Well, you did say we weren't allowed to decorate the car so I had to find something to attach all the stuff I'd got!

Today has been a great day and I've never seen Harry look happier – well, not since he visited the Turkish baths, anyway. And he has good reason to feel pleased with himself, as today he's just married a beautiful woman and learnt how to tie a cravat.

I would like to finish by wishing you both all the very best for your future together and to end with this insightful quote: 'If you have love, you don't need to have anything else, and if you don't have it, it doesn't matter much what else you have'. And it's clear from how happy you both look today that you don't need anything else. So, ladies and gentlemen, would you please be upstanding and raise your glasses for a toast: to the bride and groom.

WEDDING SPEECH No. 6

Good afternoon, ladies and gentlemen. You might be interested to hear that on this day in 1959, the Russian *Luna 1* was the first rocket to go past the moon. Imagine the discussion that went on if it was a husband-and-wife pilot and navigation team on board … 'Great, we missed it … I told you we should have turned left back there'.

My name is Tom and I'm Harry's best man. People have asked me what sort of reaction I had to being asked. Well, I think you'd best describe it as an allergic one. First, there was the rash, then the shaking and the severe headaches (although I did discover later that the rash was caused by something else). My emotional reaction was not so good, either. Obviously, I kept asking 'Why me?', and I expect I wasn't the only one asking that question. But I appreciate it's a great honour … for Harry to have me here today, and of course for me to have been chosen as his best man.

I'd first like to say how gorgeous Emily is looking and to thank you, Harry, on behalf of the bridesmaids for their gifts, who I might add are also looking fantastic. And speaking of gifts, I do like it that nowadays for the wedding present you can just call the number that comes with the invite and pick something. When I rang up, I was impressed that the list was being held at American Golf – I didn't think Emily could go any higher in my estimation – although I soon realised that I'd pressed redial on my phone by mistake. When I finally got through to the right place, I wanted to make sure they had everything they needed in their new house … for the guest bedroom. Clearly a lot of you had the same idea, as those items had already gone, but due to an oversight they had left the guest bedroom mini-bar off the list so I ordered one of those instead. And it gets better, as do you know what it came with? By the way, when I asked my wife she said, 'Hopefully the receipt', which was a bit disappointing, particularly as the shop would give me a discount if I ordered a second one. But actually what it did come with was a complete set of miniatures, so my advice is to book early if you're thinking of visiting.

Harry told me as best man I'd play a key role in the day's proceedings. I don't wish to gripe, but based on the important role I'm playing today, I was slightly disappointed in the vestry earlier that there wasn't some sort of certificate for me as well. Don't get me wrong, I don't begrudge Emily and Harry getting theirs – I can see their role today is also important. By the way I would like to apologise for the time we spent in the vestry but unfortunately the Internet was down so we had to wait before Emily and Harry could update their Facebook status.

So is there a quote that nicely describes Harry? Well, I think I found one. It's from Spock, not Dr Spock the child psychiatrist, although I'm sure he would have found that Harry provided enough material for a whole conference. No, this is the other Spock, second in command of the starship *Enterprise*, who said to Captain Kirk, 'It's life, Jim, but not as we know it.'

It was sixteen years ago when Harry first asked me to be his friend, and after the offer of some sweets, the deal was done. Don't know if you had the same offer, Emily? I do wonder how Harry made such a good catch as Emily. Anyway it seems persistence played its part – I think he just wore Emily down. In the end they came to a deal that she would go out with him on a date if he let go of her ankles. I did ask Emily what she thought of him after that first date, expecting the normal response from previous dates. Either: 'Does he always eat just with a spoon?' or 'How come he's so annoying?' Practice, by the way, is the answer. But actually she said what a great guy he was. I would also agree that Harry is a pretty good bloke, although I did think that was simply because I am such a poor judge of character. But here was someone else who thought the same as me and I think Emily and I have been friends ever since.

Harry was actually pretty popular at school, but a lot of that was perhaps due to the British way of sympathising with the underdog. He was multi-talented at sport and turned out for both the rugby and cricket teams … when they were short of players. Harry did OK academically as well and left with a broad range of grades and a personal message from the headmaster – 'Don't come back'. He still tries to keep in touch with his old classmates; admittedly this has been made difficult since he moved away and also because of attempts by them to block him from having access to the Friends Reunited website.

As well as sport, Harry also has more cultured interests. In particular, he enjoys wine and does seem to know quite a lot about it, so you will be pleased to hear that last weekend he uncorked and sampled all the bottles you've drunk here today and they were all fine. I did ask if he also opened and tested the champagne, but he said of course not as it would have gone flat by now. See, he knows his stuff.

And hopefully your champagne is still bubbly for I'd now like to ask you to raise your glasses and toast the happy couple: to Emily and Harry.

WEDDING SPEECH No. 7
Good afternoon, ladies and gentlemen. Some of the wedding etiquette books suggest that you start the best man's speech by

referring to what other famous events took place on this day. Well, I've had a look, and on 19 January 1915 German Zeppelins attacked England for the first time, and, rather unusually, they chose the holiday resort Great Yarmouth as their target. I guess once in sight of the sun-loungers, they just dropped out a load of beach towels.

When Harry asked me to be his best man I think he tried to soften me up by telling me that he'd set remarkably tough criteria in the selection process – by which I guess he meant it had to be someone who liked him. Anyway, luckily on that count I pass with distinction, as he is a great friend and it's an honour for me to be here today as his best man. I'm also very pleased he's marrying Emily. They do say opposites attract, and seeing how beautiful Emily is looking today, I'd have to agree. And of course the bridesmaids are looking fantastic as well, and, on their behalf, I'd like to thank you, Harry, for the lovely gifts you have given them.

I know you'll all agree with me that it's been a great day and a large part of the success is due to Emily and her mum, who have been heavily involved in the organisation. Harry has played his part even after a shaky start when he was given the job of arranging the flowers for the wedding – well, not the actual flower arranging itself, that would be a creative disaster. No, just ordering them. But when Emily heard, let's just say she was a bit disappointed and, surprisingly, not so excited as Harry about the 5p-off-a-litre deal which came with the purchase, but not so disappointed as the garage was to lose their first ever wedding order and to hear that Harry was also having second thoughts about the car accessory favours, which basically just left Emily's L plates for the hen party on order.

I think Harry would have been pleased just to have L plates as his accessories on the stag do. As you know, there is a stag party rule along the lines of what happens in Vegas, stays in Vegas – but as we didn't go to Vegas, I think I can fill you in a bit. As we were staying locally, the evening in town was sorted so all we had to do was arrange the daytime activity. Harry said he didn't mind what we did on the stag do so long as it was something he was good at. Now that's what you call starting with a blank piece of paper! Anyway after a week of thinking we were in danger of having to spend the whole day playing Junior Cluedo, so we relaxed the criteria to include things he hadn't done before and this is where the fact that Harry has done so little in his life really helped: we were spoilt for choice. So in the end we went for paintballing. We then had to decide what role to give Harry in our combat force. Well, they do say play to your strengths ... but what if that person hasn't got any? Well, as we all know from experience, those people tend to be given the senior management roles and, true to form, our stag team did pretty well with General Harry in command. I think in part this was due to the confusion caused in the enemy ranks by the sight of the opposing forces approaching led by a giant chicken wielding an inappropriate inflatable.

This isn't a one-off leadership success story either. Harry has been very successful in life generally, and it's not just me saying that ... he himself says it all the time. He'd definitely make the list of the one hundred most successful people . . . that I know. Harry has certainly been successful at work and over the years has gained the respect of his colleagues, but I think they see him as quite a serious person so I thought it might be nice for them to see his lighter side, which is why I've submitted the stag party photos for inclusion in their staff newsletter.

Anyway you don't need to think about work for a while as you have your honeymoon to look forward to. On the subject of honeymoons, I know all couples come back saying they had a brilliant time, but I'm not so sure: if they're that good, why don't they ever go on another one? But I'm sure you'll both have great fun on yours, particularly as I've bought you a book to take with you that should explain everything and save you any embarrassment or misunderstanding. It did come with a DVD as well, but I've kept that for my own reference. It's a Spanish phrase book [get phrase book out of bag]. I'll just highlight a couple of phrases that you might find useful, Harry. '¿A què hora es el espectaculo?' – 'What time is the floor show?' You might remember that one from the stag do. And 'Por favor las entradas mas baratas' – 'The cheapest seats, please.'

I think I'm also supposed to give the newlyweds some advice. Well, I thought I'd look at people who've been together for a long time and see what I could glean. I found a partnership that's lasted over fifty years and I think it works because they have mutual respect for each other and do their own thing, but when they do come together, they're at their best. I am of course talking about the Rolling Stones and I thought this was particularly appropriate since Harry has recently made his own positive contribution to the music world by finally giving up playing the guitar. So, ladies and gentlemen, on that inspirational musical note could I please ask you to be upstanding, raise your glasses and join me in a toast: to Mr and Mrs Wright, the bride and groom.

WEDDING SPEECH No. 8

Good afternoon, ladies and gentlemen. First, I'd like to thank you for that warm welcome, as when I asked Harry what sort of reception I'd get, he said it probably wouldn't be great. In fact, he said it might be better if I stayed outside – which was a bit worrying until I realised he was talking about making mobile phone calls. But I was still a bit nervous this morning and I wasn't the only one, as Harry fell back on his only real vice (smoking) and, with the nerves, he got through a few cigarettes. I did manage to stop him lighting up in the church, even though, as he pointed out, there weren't any 'no smoking' signs up! I get the feeling Harry's not a regular in church and certainly not for weddings, as after Emily said her vows, I'm sure I heard him say 'Bank' to the vicar. By the way, Harry, I know you were a bit confused when you heard about couples renewing their vows, so just to confirm, that's optional. Now you can stop worrying about the renewal forms getting lost in the post, or more likely Emily hiding them!

I know some of you have had a sweepstake for the length of my speech and I assume Harry was the one who chose just thirty seconds, always the optimist. I was slightly concerned to hear rumours that there was a second sweepstake being run for the number of guests still in the room by the end of my speech, though. However, at the risk of losing some of the audience straight away I'm going to start with a four-letter word: love. Particularly as a lot of you will know that Harry has a history of finding himself in desperate love situations ... when he's playing tennis, so it's good to know that with Emily, who is also a keen tennis player, he's finally found the perfect love match: a faultless mixed doubles pairing.

I've chosen three words to describe Emily and Harry – attractive, charming and intelligent. Those are obviously the three words for Emily, who I'd like to add is looking fantastic today in her wedding dress. Harry did ask me yesterday what Emily would be wearing. I said I didn't know but she'd definitely be in white, to which he replied, 'Why, have we got a match later on?' Anyway, three words to describe Harry: a bit odd. So it was quite an achievement to persuade Emily to marry him and they celebrated their engagement by going away for the weekend. Emily found a lovely little hotel in the Cotswolds ... pretty good going, working within the budget Harry had given her. And they have been almost inseparable ever since, although Harry did tell me that once he was married, he would still be going to the singles night at the local club in town. I don't know why, as he's never been successful in the past – in fact the furthest he's ever got in the club's singles tournament is the quarter-finals.

Congratulations, Emily, in taking on one of the males of the species today. You're probably slightly concerned that he didn't come with some sort of instruction manual. Not to worry, as he's pretty simple to operate and to help with that, I have the controls here [get out TV remote control]. If you do have a problem getting any sense out of him, try switching channels. This particular model comes with ten conversational channels, although nine of them are sport and the other one is the adult channel (there's no possibility either of upgrading this one to include arts and culture). I'm afraid you will also find that a lot of what you hear will be repeats. Still, if that begins to get a bit boring I see there is at least a mute button.

Before I finish, I thought I'd look to the future and talk about anniversaries as I found a list in one of the etiquette books. I hadn't realised that all the anniversaries have something associated with them. So, Harry, I thought I'd let you know the first few so you can get a relevant present for Emily sorted out well in advance. Your first anniversary is the paper one, and remembering your artistic abilities at school, I think origami is definitely a non-starter but something created from papier-mâché could work. Your second anniversary is the cotton one, and with your fashion sense as long as you don't buy Emily any clothes, you'll be fine. And I know you'll have fun thinking up your own idea for your third anniversary because that's the leather one. Then your fourth anniversary is your fruit or flowers one. By the way, if you do give flowers, just be careful: I remember once giving flowers to a girlfriend and getting a very frosty reception at her front door. 'But I thought those were your favourites?' I said. 'Yes, they are,' she told me, 'and that's why I planted them.' Also, you'll probably want to go somewhere to celebrate. Rather than making it a surprise, do discuss it with Emily first ... just in case she wants to go with you!

I think you'll agree that with all these different anniversaries to celebrate they both have a lot to look forward to, so I'd like to finish now by wishing Emily and Harry all the very best for their future together and could I ask everyone to please be upstanding to join me in raising a glass as I'd like to propose a toast: to Emily and Harry, the bride and groom.

Finally, I have just one or two cards to read out [read out messages]. Here is one from David Cameron and Nick Clegg, wishing you all the best, and their advice for a great partnership is never to discuss politics in the bedroom ... and both their marriages have lasted a long time, so sound advice!

WEDDING SPEECH No. 9

Good afternoon, ladies and gentlemen. I thought you might be interested to know that according to government statistics there are over 250,000 weddings in the UK every year, which means today alone there are probably a good few thousand taking place. That's a lot of best man's speeches so I'm very pleased that so many people have chosen to come here to listen to mine, even though I noticed my name was absent from your wedding invitations but I guess word has just got round.

So, as you probably know, my name is Tom and I have to say up to now I've enjoyed being best man. One of the most enjoyable bits is seeing all the planning but not actually having to do very much. My only input was suggesting maybe they should consider having a pagan wedding as I had read that there was no best man's speech required, although I did say to Harry that if they went for that option to make sure he remembered to tick the 'no live sacrifices' box as that was one duty I wasn't prepared to perform.

Watching the organisation I've seen that one of the hardest bits is preparing the seating plan. I guess this is necessary as there are always a few members of the older generation attending weddings and if you didn't have a seating plan there would be a mass scrum and some of the youngsters might get hurt. I've witnessed the ugly scenes you get in the rush for seats at a National Trust property tea rooms at 4 p.m. Emily and Harry certainly spent many hours trying to get you all seated next to someone with whom you'll have something in common and hopefully get on with – and of course on the other side you have your partner.

It was obviously a great honour to be chosen by Harry as best man. I have known him for some time and he's been a close friend. If you asked me to describe in just one word our relationship, I guess I'd have to say 'platonic', just to be clear. But he has been a very good friend over the years and we've helped each other achieve new heights, which I don't think either of us would have thought possible when we were kids – for instance, reaching the top level on many computer games. Some people have said that this just proves Harry is still a kid. I have to say I strongly disagree ... what proves it is that he still chases pigeons when we're out!

As you may know, as well as computer games, Harry is very keen on rugby. By the way, I don't know if any of you have seen the new bed he wants to get now that he's married. Here it is [show photo of a pencil post bed, where both ends look like rugby goals]. Looks familiar? If you can't see it, I'll just read the caption below. It's called 'The Twickenham' and then it says, 'where all your dreams come true' – or nightmares perhaps, Emily! I know Harry has already been looking for a green duvet cover and is keen to start sorting out positions. Although, Emily, I think you only really need to start worrying if he suggests building spectator stands!

Anyway they have the honeymoon to look forward to first. Harry said he'd make it a surprise. I was certainly surprised when he told me what he was planning, and when he asked Emily if she'd prefer a northern or southern hemisphere tour, I think the alarm bells started ringing. Anyway she has chosen the southern hemisphere tour after confirming that the rugby season is over in Australia. So, Harry, just to make sure you look the part while you're there, I've a small presentation to make [get out Aussie cork hat with 'Just Married' written on it, Fosters beer cans at the back and sprayed with shaving cream].

Harry is hoping to see lots of wildlife on the trip because he likes all animals – some people might say a little too much, and I can understand why you all seem to have left your pets at home today. Certainly, the police advice to keep your pets inside on Bonfire Night and outside when Harry's staying over seems a sensible precaution.

Harry says he likes animals because they are simple creatures and easy to understand. He does seem to be able to make a connection with them so I'm sure the feeling is mutual. In fact I imagine, Emily, that you might have a few nagging concerns about the genetic line going forward so I thought I'd offer you these reassuring words from Charles Darwin, who said 'It is not the strongest of the species that survives, nor the most intelligent, but the one most responsive to change'. And by getting married, which is a life-changing event, Harry proves that he meets all three criteria.

So what a commitment Emily has made today, taking on Harry. And remember, as the car bumper stickers say, 'A husband is for life, not just for the wedding day'.

So I'd like to finish by wishing you both the very best for your new life together. Marceline Desbordes-Valmore once described her relationship with hopefully one of her husbands (she was married twice) by saying 'Are we not like two volumes of one book?' and I know this is certainly true for Emily and Harry, although as Harry isn't a great reader perhaps two DVDs in a boxed set might be more appropriate. In fact, he told me earlier how much he is looking forward to sharing everything with Emily, which is lovely – although my advice to you, Emily, for the honeymoon is to hide your toothbrush!

So could I ask you all to please be upstanding and raise your glasses as I'd like to propose a toast: to the best man … that I know, Harry and his beautiful wife Emily; to Emily and Harry.

I'd now like to read out the messages from those who couldn't make it today [read out messages]. Here is one from David

Miliband, wishing you all the best, and he says if your brother is best man, don't let him near the wedding cake knife!

WEDDING SPEECH No. 10

Good afternoon, ladies and gentlemen. Before I start, the hotel have asked me to point out the nearest emergency exits to you – I guess they heard me practising my speech earlier on! My name is Tom and I'm the one Harry has chosen to be his best man. It's funny, at primary school I always wanted to be chosen for one of the speaking parts but if this was a school play now, a few minutes ago I would have given anything to have been chosen as table decoration number four, but then I remembered why I'm doing this: because Harry is a great friend and this is a real honour for me.

It's also a privilege to speak on behalf of the bridesmaids, who look fantastic, and to thank you, Harry, for their presents. Also, congratulations to you, Harry, as by marrying Emily, you have definitely hit the jackpot.

So, what interests does Harry have? Well, you probably know that he is a big cricket fan – I know he was a bit envious that Emily got to wear the whites today. Emily, on the other hand, isn't so keen, although Harry thinks she may be starting to show some interest as she recently said, 'What's the silly point in it?' And for those of you now looking a bit confused, hopefully there'll be a cricket fan on your table to explain that one afterwards.

But it was another sport which brought Emily and Harry together as they met at the badminton club, and, coincidentally, shuttlecocks was also the name of the specialist stag party mini-bus company we used – well, I wish it had been! It's easy to see what Harry saw in Emily when they met on court – the perfect partner – but what did she see in Harry? Room for improvement, I imagine!

Not sure if you know this, but Harry is a big movie fan so when I asked him what Emily had said when he asked her out, he just said, '*Jerry Maguire*'. Well, there are two famous lines from that film if you remember: one was said by Renée Zellweger to Tom Cruise after his long romantic speech and that was 'you had me at hello' and the other one was 'show me the money' – and I still can't decide which one is the more likely response from someone Harry has just asked out. Anyway, happily and surprisingly, Emily said yes and I have to say, they are very well matched. They definitely look like a couple of film stars today. And this made me think that it would be fun, particularly as Harry's such a movie fan, to ask people which screen couple Emily and Harry resemble the most. So I did this survey earlier on and you'll be pleased to hear that the top voted couple were Humphrey Bogart and Ingrid Bergman in the most romantic film of all time: *Casablanca*. Although the only similarity I can see between Harry and Bogart's character, Rick, is that he spends almost the whole time in the bar! I was less surprised by the nominations in the animated category, where, as you'd expect, *Lady and the Tramp* and *Beauty and the Beast* featured heavily.

Harry's other main interest is cars – even as a child he was obsessed with making models of his favourite ones. In fact he was the only person I knew growing up that if you told him he'd be spending the evening with a model he'd be disappointed when she turned up, not to say how confused she would have been to be met by a guy at the door holding a selection of miniature paint pots and brushes! Although she probably sat for a few artists before, I expect none of them worked to exact 1:12 scale.

Once Harry was seventeen and got to drive for himself, he found out that it was even more fun when the car had a real engine. In fact, judging by the way he drives, I think he must assume that getting points on your licence works a bit like supermarket loyalty cards or air miles. Don't worry, Emily, his penalty points are one thing he won't be asking you to share with him now you're married – even MPs know that's not a good idea. Although he won't be breaking any speed limits when you set off for the honeymoon this evening, not with all the stuff tied to the car and shaving cream all over the windows. In fact you'll be lucky to get out of the car park!

I should finish now before Harry makes a dash for the car, and so I'll leave you with these words of wisdom from Ogden Nash, who once said: 'To keep your marriage brimming, with love in the loving cup, whenever you're wrong, admit it; whenever you're right, shut up'. And before I finally shut up, I'd just like to offer my congratulations and to wish you both all the very best for your future together. And now could I ask everyone to please be upstanding and raise your glasses for a toast: to Mr and Mrs Wright, the bride and groom.

I'd now like to read out a few messages from some friends who couldn't be here today [read out messages]. The final one is from Clarkson, Hammond and May, which at first I thought was Harry's solicitors putting a gagging order on my speech. But actually it's the *Top Gear* team wishing you all the best and thanking you for your suggestion for a new feature, 'Groom in a Reasonably Priced Saloon', which they will consider once they stop laughing at the photo of your car which you sent in. Which is a bit harsh as it's not even a Peugeot, although it could have been, but Harry was worried that if he bought a French car then he wouldn't understand the Sat-Nav directions. And on that bombshell, goodnight!

8. DELIVERING THE SPEECH

8.1 PRACTISE

This chapter gives guidance on how to ensure that you deliver a great speech on the day. A key element of your preparation will be practising the speech. The more you practise, the better you will get at delivering it. This will help ensure that on the day you speak clearly, avoid using distracting gestures, get the timing right, and know the speech well enough to be able to rely only on notes. It's a good idea to practise the speech standing up because this is how you will be delivering it. You should also time the speech; although, as mentioned in Chapter 6, there are no set rules for the length of a best man's speech something between five and ten minutes is usually about right. As you practise you will notice that your confidence grows, and feeling confident in your ability to deliver a great speech will be a big factor in being successful on the day.

8.2 COMMITTING TO MEMORY

Most people will start practising a speech by reading out loud the full version. However, on the wedding day itself you should try to avoid reading the speech out word for word as it is likely to sound unnatural and lack fluency. Also, if you are looking down at the speech most of the time you will find it difficult to engage with your audience. So, once you have practised it out loud a few times, prepare some note cards with key words and phrases relating to each part of the speech written on them. Choose your words and phrases carefully; they should immediately remind you of what to say when you look at them. You should then move on to practising the speech with just these in your hand, but keep the full version of the speech nearby for reference.

Once you have your note cards, keep practising and you will find that you need to refer to the notes less and less. In fact you may not need to refer to the note cards at all during your speech; they are really just there as prompts if you need them. This method of delivering the speech is a bit like giving a PowerPoint presentation with the bullet points on the slides guiding you through. Every time you give the presentation it will be slightly different because although you know it well, you haven't gone so far as to memorise it.

As the speech is reasonably short you could go one step further and memorise it all, word for word. Having spent a lot of time getting the wording of the speech just right, it's a pity not to then deliver it the same way. If you intend to recite it from memory you will need to have practised it a lot to be able to deliver it in a way that sounds natural, like an actor in a play. You don't want to sound as if you are reading from an invisible script. One drawback of this method is a lack of flexibility, making it more difficult to incorporate last-minute anecdotes from the day without potentially throwing you off-track.

Whether memorising the speech in full or using note cards, on the day itself you should still have a copy of the speech with you. It's very unlikely that you will need it, but it's good to know that it's there just in case, which in itself will reduce the chances of you actually needing to refer to it.

8.3 OVERCOMING NERVES

The main way to reduce nerves on the day is to make sure that you have done as much preparation beforehand as possible. The more confident you are that you have written a great speech and have nailed the delivery, the less nervous you will be. Being realistic though, however much preparation you have done you will probably still be feeling quite nervous. However, a few nerves are a good thing as you need a bit of an adrenalin rush when you get up to speak, as you have to be alert. Remember, the fear of giving the speech is many times worse than the actual delivery.

Other than being well prepared, what else can you do to calm any nerves on the day? The obvious answer is to drink excessive amounts of alcohol, and there will certainly be an opportunity with all the wine on the table. Then you won't be nervous at all when you get up to speak, neither unfortunately will you be very coherent, although on the plus side your drunken ramblings will probably be an instant hit on YouTube. However, having one swift drink for a bit of Dutch courage before you get up to give your speech is fine, so long as you think you can keep a clear head and stick to just the one drink. Ideally you should leave the drinking to the guests until after you have finished the speech, though.

One way of reducing how nervous you feel on the day is to remember the things you have working in your favour. First, everyone is in a celebratory mood and enjoying themselves and you are among friends, quite a few of whom will have had a few drinks themselves so they will be ready to laugh. Of course you may get the odd heckler, but at a wedding this is normally very light-hearted, so if that happens just smile and carry on.

So the audience is on your side and willing you to succeed. Everyone knows what a nerve-wracking experience it is to give a best man's speech so you already have their sympathy. This means that any weak attempt at corny humour will get a laugh – no one expects a quality stand-up comedy routine. Although we talk up the best man's speech, most people attending weddings go with pretty low expectations of it. This makes things a lot easier, so that if you actually do come out with something genuinely funny the audience will probably fall off their chairs, if not due to laughing, certainly in surprise. These are perfect conditions for delivering a speech.

Finally, the guests will have just sat through a couple of warm-up acts to get them ready for the main event. The speeches by the father of the bride and the groom are perfect in this respect, as neither of them is intended to be funny so you won't be upstaged, but they will probably have a bit of humour in them so the audience will have had some practice laughing. The stage will therefore be perfectly set for you to make your entrance. Before getting up to speak you will probably want to take a sip of water as your mouth may be dry, and a couple of deep breaths to calm the nerves. However, once you get going, and particularly after you get your first laugh, you will be surprised at how relaxed you feel.

8.4 NATURAL DELIVERY

Aim to deliver the speech in a smooth, flowing and conversational style. As it's a personal speech you want it to feel intimate, as if you were telling it to a small group of close friends in the pub. Having said that, you do need to be heard at the back, so make sure you speak up loudly enough for everyone to hear you. This is not about shouting but being able to turn up the volume a bit. More generally you should use your voice as effectively as possible while giving the speech. Imagine a speech given in a monotone voice with no variety in pitch, tone or volume, and you can see just how important it is to use these variations to make your speech as entertaining as possible. Try to pronounce your words clearly and avoid too many ers and ums (unless you are using them intentionally for comic pauses; see comic timing, page 146). Make a conscious effort to speak slowly as there is a tendency, without realising it, to talk faster when giving a speech. Also, the speech should sound like you speaking, so don't put on a different speech voice; people know you and need to recognise the speaker as the person they know.

You might consider recording your speech, which allows you to hear how you sound, and if it's a video recording you can check your body language at the same time, which is discussed in detail below.

8.5 BODY LANGUAGE

Posture does matter when public speaking: you look a lot better and more confident if you stand up straight and don't slouch. Also, it's a lot easier to project your voice that way. Try to avoid any distracting mannerisms such as swaying backwards and forwards or playing with coins in your pocket or a ring on your finger; you can spot these by either video recording yourself or just practising the speech in front of a mirror. Hand gestures are fine if you are emphasising a point, but if it's just wild gesticulating of your whole arms for no apparent reason then it becomes a distraction. But there is no need to do the opposite and stand rigidly still; some body movement will make the speech feel lively and help your interaction with the audience. This is an entertaining speech and if you watch comedians doing stand-up routines there tends to be a lot more movement than, say, a politician giving a speech. Comedians will also make more use of facial expressions, including the most important one: smiling. This is something you should be doing throughout your speech; you need to look as though you are enjoying the experience, which hopefully you will be. If you seem to be having fun it will be contagious.

Finally, you can help to make a strong connection with the audience by looking up and making eye contact with the guests as you are speaking. Not staring, you don't want to frighten anyone; just move your gaze around the room making eye contact with people as you do so.

8.6 COMIC TIMING

The best man's speech is probably different from any other speech you will give in your life as it needs to be both personal and amusing. This is possibly why even the most accomplished public speakers will feel nervous about giving one. Generally it's the funny bit that most people worry about being able to pull off. Not only do you have to think of something that the guests will find funny, which is hard enough with such a range of people in the audience, you then have to have the confidence to say it and in a way that makes them laugh. It's certainly true that some people are better than others at telling amusing stories, but just as there are very few brilliant raconteurs around, there are also very few people who are unable to say anything funny. That leaves 99 per cent of us in the middle, who, given enough time to prepare and a bit of courage, can stand up and say something that will get a laugh.

Unfortunately it's very easy to kill off a potentially amusing story either by getting the wording or the timing wrong. The wording of the speech has already been discussed in Chapter 6 so here we will assume you now have the right words and focus on timing. We all know from watching comedians on TV that timing in comedy is crucial. In fact a good way to gain an understanding of just how timing works is to watch how the best professional comedians do it. To get the timing right it's important to practise saying a joke or anecdote out loud, as you need to be able to hear it. This is mainly about getting the rhythm and pace right and it's a process of trial and error.

The other aspect of timing that is important for comedy is the use of pauses. Pausing at the relevant moment allows you to build suspense to get everyone ready for the punch line. You can also use pauses if you wish to allude to what you might be thinking about saying next but can then go on to talk about something else. If you don't like the idea of the silence during a pause you can always fill it by saying 'er' or 'um'.

As an example I have reproduced part of the Archery speech from Chapter 6 (page 94) below and added where I think an extra-long pause should be taken in addition to the normal pauses that you would expect to have at the commas and end of sentences.

'As you know, Harry was into archery from an early age [show painting of naked Cupid with Harry's face]*; here he is as a baby showing off his* PAUSE *bow and arrows ...*

... So to compensate for no flypast today, for the pre-evening entertainment you'll be pleased to hear that I've brought along my bow and arrows, and PAUSE *some apples. For the benefit of any children who don't know the story of* William Tell, *it's all pretty straightforward. You put the apple on your head, your parents sign a disclaimer, and I then shoot the arrow at the apple. If I miss,* PAUSE *you get to keep the apple. I can see some of you are beginning to look worried, but there's no need –* PAUSE *there are plenty of apples to go round. Although a word of advice: try to get one of my early slots before the alcohol starts to kick in'.*

One final thing is that you will of course also need extra-long pauses after your punch lines while you wait for everyone to stop laughing, as you don't want them to miss what you say next.

8.7 FINAL WORDS

I hope you found this chapter helpful in your preparations for delivering your speech and that the book overall has provided you with useful guidance on how to carry out all your duties as best man. I am confident that you will enjoy the whole experience both before and on the wedding day; and also afterwards when you look back, knowing you were such a big part of making it a great day for everyone. On a personal level, as someone who has been through it all, I am slightly envious as I know that in particular on the wedding day, once the speech is over, you are going to have a fantastic time for the rest of the evening; the pay-off is definitely worth all the hard work you are currently putting in. So enjoy it and good luck!

APPENDIX – STAG PARTY ONLINE RESOURCES

Below is a selection of online resources that you may find useful when planning your stag party.

STAG PARTY ORGANISERS

Chillisauce Experiences – www.chillisauce.co.uk

Last Night of Freedom – www.lastnightoffreedom.co.uk

StagWeb – www.stagweb.co.uk

The Stag Company – www.thestagcompany.com

UK ACTIVITY CENTRES

Central – Garlands – www.garlandsleisure.co.uk

Northeast – The Camp Hill Estate – www.camphill.co.uk

Northwest – Holmescales Activity Centre – www.holmescales.com

Southeast – Qleisure Corporate Entertainment – www.qleisure.co.uk

Southwest – Mendip Outdoor Pursuits – www.mendipoutdoorpursuits.co.uk

Northern Ireland – Todds Leap – www.toddsleap.com

Scotland – Nae Limits – www.naelimits.co.uk

Wales – Adventure Britain – www.adventurebritain.com

UK ACTIVITY PROVIDERS/ ORGANISATIONS

Archery – Archery GB – www.archerygb.org

Clay Pigeon Shooting – Clay Pigeon Shooting Association – www.cpsa.co.uk

Five-a-side Football – Goals Soccer Centres – www.goalsfootball.co.uk

Go-karting – National Karting Association – www.nationalkarting.co.uk

Golf – UK Golf Guide – www.ukgolfguide.com

Greyhound racing – Greyhound Board of Great Britain – www.thedogs.co.uk

High Ropes – Go Ape! – www.goape.co.uk

Horse racing – The Racecourse Association Limited – www.britishracecourses.org

Kite Surfing – British Kitesports Association – www.britishkite surfingassociation.co.uk

Motorsports – TrackDays.co.uk (booking agent) – www.trackdays.co.uk

Paintballing – UK Paintball Sports Federation – www.ukpsf.com

Scuba diving – British Sub-Aqua Club – www.bsac.com

Surfing – Surfing GB –
http://surfinggb.com

Various activities – Go Ballistic
(booking agent) –
www.theactivitypeople.co.uk

Water Skiing & Wakeboard – British
Water Ski & Wakeboard –
www.bwsw.org.uk

Waterways Boat Hire – Canal & River
Trust – www.canalrivertrust.org
(England and Wales); Scottish
Canals – www.scottishcanals.co.uk;
Waterways Ireland (including
Northern Ireland) –
www.waterwaysireland.org.

FLIGHTS AND ACCOMMODATION

Agoda – www.agoda.com

Booking.com – www.booking.com

easyJet – www.easyjet.com

ebookers.com – www.ebookers.com

Expedia.co.uk – www.expedia.co.uk

Kayak – www.kayak.co.uk

Ryanair – www.ryanair.com

Skyscanner – www.skyscanner.net

TripAdvisor – www.tripadvisor.co.uk

ACCESSORIES

Last Night of Freedom –
www.lastnightoffreedom.co.uk

StagsandHens.com –
www.stagsandhens.com (this
website also has a directory of stag
party service providers)

The Stag Company –
www.thestagcompany.com

INDEX